Spiritual Growl

HEALING YOUR INNER CHILD
A Guide into Shadow Work

MONIQUE JOINER SIEDLAK

Oshun
Publications

Healing Your Inner Child: A Guide into Shadow Work © Copyright 2021 by Monique Joiner Siedlak

ISBN: 978-1-950378-93-7

All rights reserved

The content contained within this book may not be reproduced, duplicated or transmitted without direct written permission from the author or the publisher.

Under no circumstances will any blame or legal responsibility be held against the publisher, or author, for any damages, reparation, or monetary loss due to the information contained within this book, either directly or indirectly.

Legal Notice

This book is copyright protected. It is only for personal use. You cannot amend, distribute, sell, use, quote or paraphrase any part, or the content within this book, without the consent of the author or publisher.

Disclaimer Notice

Please note the information contained within this document is for educational and entertainment purposes only. All effort has been executed to present accurate, up to date, reliable, complete information. No warranties of any kind are declared or implied. Readers acknowledge that the author is not engaged in the rendering of legal, financial, medical or professional advice. The content within this book has been derived from various sources. Please consult a licensed professional before attempting any techniques outlined in this book.

By reading this document, the reader agrees that under no circumstances is the author responsible for any losses, direct or indirect, that are incurred as a result of the use of the information contained within this document, including, but not limited to, errors, omissions, or inaccuracies.

Cover Design by MJS

Cover Image by ra2studio@depositphotos.com

Published by Oshun Publications

www.oshunpublications.com

Books in the Series

Spiritual Growth and Personal Development
Creative Visualization
Astral Projection for Beginners
Meditation for Beginners
Reiki for Beginners
Manifesting With the Law of Attraction
Being an Empath Today
Crystal Healing: A Beginner's Guide to Natural Healing
Communicating with Your Spirit Guides

Contents

Introduction	xi
1. Understanding the Shadow Self	1
2. Understanding the Inner Child	7
3. What Is Shadow Work?	15
4. The Repressed Shadow Self	21
5. Identifying the Shadow Self	29
6. How to Unveil the Shadow Self	37
7. Understanding The Subconscious Mind	47
8. The Shadow Self and Projection	53
9. Facing Your Shadow Self	59
10. Healing Shadow Wounds	65
11. Shadow Work Exercises	73
12. Nurturing the Inner Child	83
Conclusion	89
References	91
About the Author	95
More Books by Monique	97
Last Chance	99
Thank You!	101

Introduction

Welcome to your comprehensive guide to shadow work. Congratulations on taking this step towards healing the shadow side of yourself. Healing isn't easy. To heal ourselves, we must embrace all of us, whether we perceive them as good or bad. It takes a lot of courage to look deep into ourselves and admit that there are things that we may not like and want to change; it can be messy and painful, but it's also beautiful. As humans, our healing work is never done because we are never finished learning. Taking the time to heal yourself — especially the parts of yourself that you would rather ignore — is what allows us to understand ourselves better. When we know ourselves, we understand the world around us better. When we realize that our healing is never done, we reach acceptance. We can release the pressures and expectations and recognize that it's a life-long process. It is meant to be enjoyed as we discover more and more about ourselves and the world around us. This book will help you to enjoy the journey of becoming conscious of your shadow self and provide you with the knowledge and the confidence to heal it. Ultimately, your shadow self is a part of you that you have hidden from yourself long ago. Facing this part of you and learning to embrace it will help empower you, set you free, and feel whole.

When we think of the word 'shadow,' we think of darkness, and this can be scary; however, there is absolutely nothing to be scared of. The point of shadow work is to shine a light on the shadows to come to the surface to be healed. You have this light within you. We all do. You're a beautiful soul full of life force energy, which gives you the power to heal yourself. You will learn that your shadow self is simply a part of you — usually created in childhood — that you have repressed. Your shadow self is not bad or wrong, and it's not an evil part of you; it is where the pain you thought you weren't strong enough to deal with goes. However, you're strong enough, and you only give power to your shadow by ignoring it. Having negative attachments to your emotions holds you back and stops you from living a full life. Shadow work allows you to love every single part of yourself, whether you see it as good or bad. Not everybody feels the need to do this in their lifetime. Still, when you're brave enough to go deeper into your healing journey, your life will improve in so many ways. So before we dive in, give yourself a big hug for getting this far.

ONE

Understanding the Shadow Self

"Until you make the unconscious conscious, it will direct your life, and you will call it fate" (Jung, 2018).

The Origin of the Shadow Self

THE SHADOW SELF IS A TERM THAT WAS COINED BY A SWISS Psychiatrist named Carl Jung (Othon, 2017). He referred to the place in your psyche where the unconscious and repressed parts of your identity are stored. You may be wondering if you have a place like this in your psyche, and the answer is yes, everyone does. You're just not conscious of it. The idea is that if you can become aware of your shadow self and integrate it into your being, you will be more balanced and live a full, rounded life. The shadow self is perceived as bad, but that isn't necessarily the case. It appears to be a negative attribute because it can harm your life by attracting some negative patterns: experiences and traumas when you aren't aware of it. You may have habitual reactions to certain people and situations. Or you may find yourself repeating the same patterns again and again and never learning your lesson. You'll never know the lesson until you can become aware of your shadow self. The shadow houses all of your unconscious fears and insecurities. As long as you remain blocked from them, you cannot react differently, learn your lesson, and heal the pain. Integrating the shadow is essential because we cannot eliminate it. All we can do is bring those aspects of ourselves out of the shadow and into the light to be accepted and healed.

Since you're a light being made up of energy, all you need to do is become conscious of the shadow and show it some love to help you instead of hindering you. After all, what happens when we shine a light on the shadows? They disappear. And you, my friend, are that light. The shadow self affects your energy body as well as your psyche. This means that if you have a trait that you have pushed down into your shadow self, and you're not aware of it, it still exists in your energy field. You will attract nervous energy, negative experiences, and chaos in your life to align with those attributes in your shadow self and prove your fears right. However, through consciousness and acceptance of those hidden fears, you can release the need for these experiences and prove to yourself that your worries are much smaller than they seem. Are you ready to prove your fears wrong?

Keep in mind that there may also be some good things hidden within your shadow self, such as gifts that you're afraid to use or talents that you no longer have confidence in, so it's not all bad. You may have rejected artistic, emotional, or spiritual parts of yourself that you were afraid to show to the world for fear of rejection. That sounds silly, right? You were afraid of being rejected, so you rejected yourself. Well, unfortunately, that is a prevalent psychological defense mechanism that all humans use at some point to protect themselves. Maybe you were a sensitive soul, and your peers weren't. Somewhere along the way, you told yourself that being unique was wrong, and so you rejected that part of yourself so that you could fit in. You have been storing things in your shadow self since childhood. It's like opening a box of old possessions.

Some of them are useless. Such as fears and insecurities, and some of them are hidden gems and valuable tools that will help you to live your life better. Such as hidden talents that you were afraid to show to the world. Your job is to open this old dusty box and shine your light on it so that you can sort through it. Once you do, it will stop banging around upstairs, getting in the way. The shadow self is like the box in this way because it's always there in the background. Responsible for all of your unconscious thought patterns, behaviors, and reactions. It's time to sort out the box, become aware of how it is running on autopilot behind the scenes, and stop it so that you are in full conscious control of your life.

Please be gentle with yourself throughout this process. Be kind to yourself as you discover what is hidden inside your unconscious shadow box. Be patient as you learn to embrace the parts of yourself that you had previously rejected. The part of you that whispers, 'you can't do it before we've even started. That's part of your shadow self. Send this part of your love! Think of yourself as a child learning a new topic for the first time. The intention is everything, and if you want to do this, you most definitely can do it.

How the Shadow Self Is Formed

Your shadow self is usually born in your childhood. As you're growing and learning, you start to become aware of the differences between you and the people around you. When you perceive these differences as negative, you label them as bad and reject them. Your parents, teachers, and peers project their beliefs and understanding of the world onto you when you're a child. This is normal. It's how we learn. However, when your beliefs differ from those you look up to, and you aren't taught that being unique is a good thing, you run into problems. You may begin to believe that there is something wrong with how you perceive the world or interact with other human beings. So you reject the parts of yourself that are different, pushing these parts of your identity, personality, and energy to the back of your subconscious, and thus the shadow self is born. This doesn't mean that you can neglect the responsibility of having a shadow self and blame the people who raised you on anything that goes wrong in your life. It's the opposite approach that will facilitate the healing of your shadow self. These people were doing the best they could for you. They only had their level of experience and understanding to offer. A massive step in embracing your shadow self is to take responsibility for the fact that it exists. You're the only person responsible for your emotions, fears, and insecurities in the same way that you're the only person responsible for healing them. By looking at the shadow self from this perspective, it will empower you to take action. The only thing standing in the way of the best life you can imagine for yourself is you.

Although your shadow self is born in childhood, you subconsciously add to it throughout your life. Suppose you have taken the time to read this book. In that case, you're probably already in the midst of your healing journey. You have realized that healing your psyche and your energy field means that there is always something new to work on. Healing requires adopting a growth mindset and constantly striving to understand yourself better. Your shadow self is no different. Any part of you that you don't see acknowledge or accept forms a part of your shadow self. Fear is the driving force behind this subconscious defense mechanism. Fear pushes anything you reject into the shadows, whether that's a talent you're afraid to share, fear you're scared to acknowledge, or an emotion you're so scared to express. The key here is acceptance. You must accept responsibility for everything that you have pushed into the shadows. Still, it is just as important that you acknowledge that you did the best that you could at the time. Judging yourself for rejecting and repressing your past actions will only add more to the shadow self. Take a deep breath, and forgive yourself for protecting yourself is the only way that you knew how at the time. After reading this book, you will reach a new level of awareness that will allow you to integrate your shadow self with your true self and use it to live your life to the fullest. Let that sit with you for a moment, and feel the gratitude of the gift you're giving to yourself by learning about your shadow self.

Effects of Ignoring the Shadow Self

When you ignore your shadow self, it operates outside of your awareness. The unconscious beliefs that the shadow is made up of impact your behavior and life experiences negatively. The issue with this is that you may not even realize how your shadow self negatively influences your life. You may repeat patterns or behave in a certain way without even knowing why. Your subconscious mind stores every experience that you've ever had and all of your habits. It doesn't differentiate between the good and the bad ones. It only knows what happened and how it made you feel in the moment. This reaction is stored in your subconscious and triggered whenever a similar event occurs in the future. Suppose you felt anxious the first time it happened. In that case, you may subconsciously place yourself in similar situations over and over again, only to prove to yourself that you were right to feel that way. According to Tracy (https://www.briantracy.com/blog/author/brian-tracy, 2017), your subconscious mind is an unquestioning servant. It will work tirelessly to make your behavior fit into a pattern associated with your internalized thoughts and emotions. This means that your shadow self will look for situations that align with what you believe to be true. For example, if you believe that you're not worthy of love and reject that belief, it becomes part of your shadow self. You may then find yourself in a series of toxic relationships. This indicates a pattern that your shadow self is playing out to satisfy the belief that you're not worthy of love. The shadow self, like all parts of us, is vibrating on an energy frequency. The more you add to the shadow, the bigger the energy field and its influence over your life. Like all energy, it attracts similar energy. Suppose you have many negative beliefs about yourself. In that case, that could explain why the world reacts negatively to you and seemingly affirming those beliefs. Your life experiences will resonate on the same vibration as your energy field. That is why integrating your shadow self is crucial if you want to have control over your life and be the conscious creator you were born to be. If you think your shadow self may negatively impact your life, and you're just now becoming aware of it, you have nothing to fear. Once you're aware of your shadow side, you can begin working on the negative energy hidden there. Subsequently, allowing yourself to live free from the unconscious habits or patterns that have been holding you back. Sometimes, the bravest souls have the most challenging battles to fight because their light is bright enough to cut through the darkest shadow. You, my friend, are likely one of those souls if you have come this far.

TWO

Understanding the Inner Child

"So, like a forgotten fire, a childhood can always flare up again within us" (Bachelard, 1971).

THE INNER CHILD IS THE PUREST PART OF YOUR PSYCHE because it stores emotional experiences from your childhood and sees them through the lens that you saw them through at the time. Up to the age of seven, you're in an altered state of consciousness, whereby your brain is like a sponge. You want to acquire as much knowledge as you can, and so you assign the meaning that you believe to be true to certain situations. For example, if, as a five-year-old, you saw that your father was angry all the time, you may have concluded that it was your fault and that you were unworthy of love. When viewed through the lens of a child who has not had enough life experiences to understand that the father is tired and frustrated from working too hard, a wounded part of the inner child is formed from this unworthy feeling. You may have carried this belief into your adult relationships by unconsciously replaying the same story. Choosing partners who made you feel like you were unworthy of love. In this way, the wounded parts of the inner child can be damaging to us as adults.

The wounded inner child is where the shadow began initially, so it is where we must start with shadow work. The inner child's needs are the love and understanding that we never received as a child. We will cling to our subconscious beliefs until our adult self can offer our inner child the knowledge that whatever situation harmed us was never our fault. Or had anything to do with us and that we are, indeed, worthy of love. Nurturing the child within you with awareness and understanding will heal the wounded child and, therefore, start allowing your shadow to come forward to be healed. Reconnecting with your inner child and letting go of the wounded parts can offer a feeling of freedom. You will remember what it feels like to be a child, feel wonder at the world, and be excited to learn new things every day. We can allow ourselves to be joyful and carefree just for the sake of it. We can allow ourselves to be creative, curious, and let go of all of our inhibitions. If we neglect those innocent and child-like qualities as we grow older, we tend to unintentionally disconnect from ourselves. Once we embrace and nurture the part of us that wants to live each day moment-to-moment without worry or stress, we will be able to live our lives as our most authentic selves.

Sit with your inner child now by picturing yourself as your younger self. What do you need? Talk to your younger self and soothe them, reminding them that they are loved, as you would any child. That pure divine essence that was always within you will come forward, but with newfound wisdom that you didn't have as a child. When your inner child feels safe and loved, your adult self feels safe and loved. Give your inner child a big hug and tell them that everything will be ok. You will be amazed at the feelings and memories that may come up from this simple exercise.

The Shadow Self vs. the Inner Child

The inner child and the shadow self are terms that are sometimes mixed up; however, they are not interchangeable. They are deeply connected but are not the same thing, so it is essential to understand the difference.

Your inner child is the pure essence of life force energy. As a baby, you came into the world, and you were perfect (you're still perfect!); however, somewhere along the way, you stopped believing that. You stopped seeing the wonder of the world and lost your innocence. Your inner child holds the key to your most authentic and most genuine self. It is the gateway to regaining your peace and innocence. Understanding this is the secret ingredient that will elevate your shadow work. Revisiting yourself as a young child is a good start. Still, you must go back to the very beginning of your development if you wish to master inner child work and shadow work.

At some point in your early development, you started to feel the pressure of your parents' expectations for you. You may have believed that this meant you had to change who you were. This is a damaging belief, and we must look at who we were before it ever formed. Who you are is enough. Babies know this. They laugh when they are amused and cry when they are upset. They are not embarrassed to let their emotions show. They are not worried about trying something new for the first time and looking like an idiot. They understand what the most significant purpose of life is — feeling joy. When babies are happy, it radiates to everybody around them. Adults love to watch them play, grow, and learn. Why do you think this is? Perhaps it's because we have so much to learn from them. The next time you're around a baby or a young child, watch them playing and how they let their emotions come and go like waves.

Watch how they drop a toy as soon as it starts to frustrate them and move on to one that brings them joy. They are relentless joy seekers, following the joy to wherever it takes them. At some point, though, they lose this innocence. This is usually the point that they experience trauma or feel victimized. To reconnect with your inner child and follow the joy again, you must first reclaim your innocence with awareness and understanding. The moment you needed something as a child and didn't get it — such as love from a parent or inclusion from your friends — is when you first felt neglected. Your neglected inner child was the first item added to the box that contains all aspects of your shadow self.

On the other hand, your shadow self is the thing that disconnects you from your pure life force energy (or inner child). This is why it is so important to dig deep to find the moment you lost your innocence as a child. If you can figure out the very first thing that happened to make you feel neglected in childhood, you will discover the exact moment that your shadow self was born. Your shadow self is invested in protecting you and your feelings. It won't allow you to try new things outside of your comfort zone if, for example, you ever failed miserably at a new task and were criticized for it as a child. It would not allow you to meet new people and show them your true self if you were bullied as a child for being different. It will shout at you that you're doing things all wrong and then repeat the same horrible patterns for you over and over again. Whether that is in the form of bad relationships, having no friends, or constantly failing in your chosen career. The reason for this is that your shadow self has been told at some point — by you — that life is tough, and you have a reason to be fearful, sad, and lonely. If we remind ourselves that, like the rest of the unconscious mind, the shadow self is a loyal servant who will guide you towards situations that affirm your beliefs, then this makes perfect sense. Therefore, it is pointless to be angry at your shadow self or judge yourself for the views you've collected. All you can do is figure out where your most extensive trauma came from and gain an understanding of where these misguided beliefs about yourself and life came from.

Once you stop the track playing repeatedly and nurture your inner child so that the neglect you felt is explained away as a symptom of a complicated world and not evidence of your unworthiness, you will no longer find the need for situations that make you feel unworthy. Can you remember what the most significant trauma from your childhood was? Sit quietly for a moment and ask your inner child. See if you can pinpoint it. Remember that you're safe and loved. You're all grown up now, and there is no need to be scared. Offer your inner child the support that you never got back then. Pat yourself on the back for working on yourself and taking the time to reconnect with your neglected inner child. They have been waiting a long time for your love.

The Inner Child and Trauma

Everybody has had some trauma in their lives. For most of us, the first trauma occurs a few moments after birth when we are slapped on the bottom by a nurse. The following trauma might have been when your sibling was born, and you understood this to mean that you weren't enough, when in fact, your parents loved you so much that they didn't want you to be alone. Looking at situations like these now, as an adult, can help you to gain perspective and insight into why you may have perceived those things like trauma and how you can let that belief go. Usually, any trauma we encounter as a child, we deem to be our fault. Blame and guilt for things we had no control over make us feel unworthy of love, and our neglected inner child contributes to the shadow self. To understand how trauma affects the inner child and makes it feel neglected, thus adding to the shadow self, is to offer an example.

Picture a young girl, around seven years old; we will call her Sally. Sally has just moved to a new school in a small village, where she doesn't know anyone. She feels alone after leaving all of her old friends behind, and the children don't understand her at this new school. She is quite sensitive and likes to stay inside to write poetry and read books. The children at this new school have no interest in reading and would rather play outside. The town they're from doesn't have a library, and they were never encouraged to read by their parents, or teachers like Sally was. Sally finds herself being excluded, and after a while, one of the girls starts picking on her. Soon enough, the rest of the children join in. They tell her she is ugly and that her poems are stupid. Sally takes this to mean that she doesn't look as nice as the others, that she's a lousy writer, and that nobody will ever accept her for who she is. Because of these traumatic events in her past, Sally grows up suppressing her love of writing. She worries about her appearance and compares herself to others daily. She finds it hard to make friends because she can't trust anybody. Do you see how Sally's inner child experienced this trauma, felt neglected, and how her shadow self is now replaying that story in her adult life? To heal this trauma in her adult life, Sally needs to look at the situation as an adult and realize that the children only picked on her because they didn't understand her. She would recognize that the joy she felt from writing poems was too important to lose, no matter what anybody's opinion was. She would understand that she finds it hard to make friends because she chooses untrustworthy people to reaffirm the belief she formed as a child. She would realize that she was never ugly. Still, she would always feel that way if she constantly looked for things she hated about herself and compared herself to airbrushed models in magazines. By looking through the lens of an adult, Sally can pinpoint these misbeliefs that have haunted her through her childhood and into adulthood. She can begin to take action by forgiving herself for carrying these misconceptions and allow herself to heal.

Going back to revisit your childhood traumas and understanding them from a new perspective is a fantastic exercise to try before you dig into shadow work. It is not going to be easy to relive the trauma, but you must remember that you're all grown up now, and it's just a memory. It can't harm you. If you wish to try to connect with your inner child and heal your trauma, you can try the following exercise:

Sit in a quiet room and close your eyes, and ask your inner child to connect with you. Envision yourself at the age that the trauma happened. What did you look like? What emotions were you feeling at the time? Now, ask your inner child what they're missing. What is it that they need? Is it to feel loved? Is it friendship? Is it a hug? Is it to feel accepted? Wait until the answer comes to you. It may take time, but it will come to you. Imagine taking your inner child in your arms and giving them the biggest hug. Tell them that they are loved, safe, and perfect just the way they are. If those old feelings resurface, that's ok. Let them out. Cry or scream at the top of your lungs if you need to. Do whatever you need to do to release those emotions and offer yourself the support that you didn't receive at the time. When you're finished, you can thank your inner child for connecting with you and remind them that you're always there for them.

A lot of shadow work centers around love. Self-love will allow you to embrace your inner child and love freely and authentically. Showing love to the parts of yourself that never received it will heal the inner child and give you the understanding you need to do the shadow work when it's time. Inner work is not easy, but your outer world reflects your inner world. Just by reading this, you're expanding your awareness, so you're already changing your life in ways that you can't yet imagine. Well done, you.

THREE

What Is Shadow Work?

"One does not become enlightened by imagining figures of light, but by making the darkness conscious" (Jung, 2018).

SHADOW WORK ENTAILS BRINGING THE UNCONSCIOUS SHADOW self into the light to integrate it with the rest of our being and live from a more conscious state. By doing this, we offer ourselves the possibility of having complete control of our lives. We were born as the creators of our reality. We know that our thoughts and emotions affect what goes on around us. We understand that our choices can determine our future. But what about the unconscious parts of us? Well, they hold a great deal of power over us, too. The unconscious brain will play out patterns according to your beliefs, whether they impact your life positively or negatively. Shadow work is at its best when you have healed your inner child's most significant traumas. Once the shadows and the neglected inner child present themselves, you can offer them the light and love they need to come into consciousness and heal. Awareness puts you in the driver's seat of your own life. Suppose a repeating pattern or a limiting belief arises, and you're waiting patiently to spot it and offer it some love. In that case, that's all it will take to bring your shadows into the light. You can practice shadow work in many different ways, all of which will be explained later on, but take your time with this journey. Sit with your inner child and allow yourself to feel joy again. Allow yourself to be playful with this. You want to avoid spending so much time searching for your shadow self that you become engrossed in it. Let it come to you. The essence of shadow work is not searching for your shadow but connecting with your inner child so that you generate enough light and love to banish the darkness.

Benefits of Shadow Work

Shadow work can be beneficial to every area of your life, on every level of your being. It can help you to become more present and aware emotionally, mentally, energetically, and spiritually. When one aspect of our consciousness is changed, it creates a ripple effect. Suppose you heal a childhood trauma mentally by visiting the psychological reasons for that trauma and changing the core belief associated with it. In that case, you will reap the benefits emotionally, too. Then, you will feel the negative emotions related to that trauma ease, and as a result, you will feel lighter. When the heavy burden of carrying that trauma is released energetically, you will feel more in touch with yourself and your spirituality. You may even find that you feel better physically, too, if you've been storing that trauma in your physical body in the form of pain or illness. There are many reasons to invest in shadow work and endless benefits. Below are five of the most common benefits of shadow work to us as human beings. Allow yourself to get excited about all of the ways you're about to improve your life. Feeling this joy and self-love will help you connect with your inner child, raise your consciousness, and expand your light.

Free Will and Conscious Choice

Your perception of life will change once you bring your unconscious thoughts, feelings, and beliefs into your conscious awareness. Once they are conscious, they can no longer control your life without you knowing about it. This puts you in a position to choose what your reality looks like without unconscious habits getting in the way. You can get out of your comfort zone and no longer find that fear holds you back from your true potential.

Better Relationships

You may not even be aware that you have an unconscious belief that being in love is painful and complex. You may see it play out in your life with partners who cause you pain. Once you bring those beliefs into the light and offer them, love, you will find yourself choosing a partner who is perfectly aligned with your true self and your joyful inner child, rather than your shadow self. These relationships will be much more loving and nurturing compared to previous ones that you may have had.

Clarity

When you embrace your shadow self, you will unearth truths about yourself that will give you a better understanding of your life. This allows you to live in the present moment and enjoy your life. Once you can see where your core beliefs came from, it will help you to get clear on what you want and live from a place of truth.

Step Out of Negative Patterns

If there is a pattern playing out in your life repeatedly, it is likely caused by an unconscious belief that your shadow self is projecting. If part of your shadow self believes that life is hard and people are mean, you may find it hard to make friends, and life will generally be hard for you. Once you uncover what the negative belief is, the need for the pattern will fall away.

Inner Peace

Peace is the highest vibrational frequency humans can reach. It comes when you have expanded your awareness enough that you're fully conscious and accepting of yourself. Once your heart is overflowing with love for yourself and the world around you, peace will follow.

The Goal of Shadow Work

The ultimate goal of shadow work is to integrate the parts of yourself that are unconscious into your consciousness to be mindful of them. Allowing yourself to take active control and live a more fulfilling life. Be careful not to stress yourself out and add more baggage to your shadow self as you embark on shadow work. It takes patience and understanding, so go easy on yourself. You're brave enough and wise enough to heal yourself, but here are some tips regarding the goals you should be setting yourself to avoid adding more negative beliefs to the shadow. Please don't judge yourself for not healing quickly enough. Everybody heals at their own pace. We cannot rush anybody's healing journey, even our own. Our soul knows when it is time; you will feel the calling, the knowing, and a need to seek answers to questions you never knew you had. If you've come this far, it's safe to say you have experienced something like this. Well, shadow work should be seen in the same way. The goal is not to hunt your shadow down as quickly as possible and banish it from your psyche. This would only add fuel to the fire. Your shadow self is a scared child that needs nurturing. Your shadow is filled with all of the fears you have ever had and everything you're insecure about. Charging at it would do more harm than good.

The best way to approach it is gently and slowly, coaxing it out. Create so much love within yourself that your shadow self feels safe enough to be vulnerable. As we already know, it all comes back to love. Let the pressure go and just work with your inner child, and cultivate the love for yourself that you have been missing. Do things you haven't done since childhood that bring you joy, such as connecting with a friend who makes your sides split open with laughter. The more you connect with your inner child by doing the things that bring you joy and allow you to feel free, the more loving and wiser you will become. Then, and only then, will you become conscious enough to notice when your shadow comes up. It may be when you decide to paint for the first time since childhood and a little voice in your head starts telling you that you're no good at it. That's your shadow. It feels safe to come out now. It will rise, and you will know what to do. You will recognize the voice as a belief that came from a lack of self-love as a child. You will be able to work with it now using the tools provided in the later chapters of this book. That is your only job. Cultivate so much love and light within yourself, and let the shadow rise to meet you so that you can heal it.

Why Shadow Work Is Effective

Shadow work is one of the most important tools you can use in your journey to enlightenment. It involves learning how to process your emotions healthily so that they don't control you. When your inner child first felt neglected and created the shadow self, that negative emotion was put into your metaphorical shadow box. Along with the negative belief about yourself, seemingly never to be seen again, but the thing is, although you forgot all about that box and haven't been aware of it for years and years, it wasn't disappearing. At the same time, it sat in the attic, collecting dust. The emotions from that first trauma have been growing every time that you've encountered a similar situation over the years. The unconscious thought that this proves you're not good enough and the emotion associated with it was added to your metaphorical shadow box. If you never addressed your shadow self, it would expand and get bigger and bigger over time. The more stored there, the more energy it takes up in your mind and in your energy field. If it eventually took up most of your energy field, it would run rampant in every area of your life. Creating horrible situations to prove that you aren't good enough. Your shadow self can ruin your life more than your conscious thoughts, which is a recipe for disaster. So it's time to give yourself a big pat on the back for taking the time to go on this journey of self-discovery and learn how to truly integrate your shadow self into your consciousness. Everything you have read so far is taking you one step closer to living a fully conscious life.

FOUR

The Repressed Shadow Self

"Every pain, addiction, anguish, longing, depression, anger or fear is an orphaned part of us seeking joy, some disowned shadow wanting to return to the light and home of ourselves" (Nordby, 2016).

YOUR UNCONSCIOUS MIND CONTAINS REPRESSED THOUGHTS, habits, and emotions. As you go deeper into your shadow work and start looking for what you have suppressed, you will begin to unearth feelings and memories that you were completely unaware of. Repression means unconsciously blocking something from your mind, whether a memory, thought, or feeling. It is a defense mechanism that your brain uses to protect you from experiencing unpleasant emotions. Anything that you perceive as painful or uncomfortable may have been repressed by your unconscious mind. This may sound like a good thing, but the problem is that when you suppress something, you don't erase it from your mind. You're simply pushing it out of your awareness and allowing it to bubble up under the surface; it will then run your life from behind the scenes.

For example, if you have repressed a lot of anger, this anger will have been pushed to the back of your unconscious mind and become part of your shadow self. Although you may consciously avoid anger since you see it as an unpleasant emotion, you will still unconsciously attract situations that bring that repressed anger to the surface. If you have repressed your anger, you may react passively and hide your true feelings when something makes you mad; however, the anger is still there. Emotional avoidance in this way only makes the problem worse and can lead to emotional pain. If you can, first, understand why your emotions were repressed in the first place, and then work on resolving them, you can change this pattern. Your relationship with your feelings will change once you accept that you have a right to express all emotions as a human being, and none are necessarily good or bad. There is a purpose for all of your feelings. They need to be felt, processed, and then released. Allowing yourself to feel your emotions until you can process them and let them go is so much healthier for your mind, body, and soul than trying to avoid them. You deserve to express your true feelings and balance any emotional distress, and that is precisely what this book will teach you to do. Let's talk about how to spot repressed emotions and how to resolve them.

What Are Repressed Emotions?

Do you find that you don't enjoy being alone because you start to feel sad or anxious and don't know why? This could be an indication that you have some repressed emotions. You might feel perfectly fine when you're in the company of others but start to feel unsettled when you're alone for too long. This is one of the most common signs that your emotions have been repressed. They try to rise when you're alone so that they can be dealt with and released. Many people deal with this by ignoring those emotions and pushing them down. Or they avoid being alone so that they don't have space to come up, but that leaves your emotions with nowhere to go. They stay in your body and can show up in other ways until they finally get your attention. That is when repressed emotions can cause problems. Every part of your being is connected in some way. Anything that affects you on an emotional level will also affect you physically, mentally, and energetically. Repressed emotions will eat away at you and cause problems to your mental and physical health. They will fester and grow within you, adding to your shadow self and hindering your life.

According to an article on hcf.com, people who bottle up their emotions increase their risk of premature death by more than 30% and their risk of cancer by 70%. Repressed emotions can also affect your self-esteem, raise your blood pressure, and increase your risk of suffering from anxiety or depression (Cousins, 2017). When we hear these statistics, we understand how important it is to heal our repressed emotions so that they don't fester. Repressed emotions have nowhere to go and, therefore, will stay trapped in your unconscious mind, nudging you with warning signs. There is no need to panic, though. You're here, and you're ready to face your repressed emotions head-on. Below are some examples of how repressed emotions can show up in your life. Take note of any that sound familiar to you and that you may need to work on. Then we will discuss how to resolve them to show up every day as your best self with nothing holding you back.

Signs of Repressed Emotions

- You try not to cry or yell because you believe that expressing anger or sadness is wrong.
- You feel uncomfortable when other people express their emotions in front of you.

- You don't have much control over your emotions and often overreact when you don't mean to.
- You can't open up to people or form intimate connections.
- You regularly engage in self-destructive behavior such as drinking, undereating, overeating, or taking drugs.
- You experience a lot of stress and anxiety that is not directly related to anything going on in your life.
- If you're unhappy with something or someone, you keep your feelings to yourself rather than telling them.
- You constantly surround yourself with people because you don't like to be alone.
- You feel like nobody knows the real you, even though you have lots of friends and family to talk to.
- You criticize yourself and others regularly.

Resolving Repressed Emotions

As mentioned earlier, the shadow self is usually first formed in childhood. The way you deal with your emotions is formed at that point. This creates a pattern or a habit that you continue to use throughout your life anytime that an emotion pops up that you don't want to address. Looking at the way that you were taught to process your emotions can be a great help in resolving repressed emotions. For example, suppose you had caregivers that encouraged you to express both positive and negative emotions and liked to talk about their feelings. In that case, you will have developed a healthy relationship with your emotions.

On the other hand, if you were always surrounded by people who didn't like talking about their feelings and punished you for talking about yours, you may have carried that into adulthood with you. Unhealthy patterns can form later in life, too. You may be in touch with your emotions. Still, you have a partner or friend who feels uncomfortable when you express them. So you bury them down and start to create a pattern of repressing certain emotions to please them. If telling somebody close to you how you feel has ever resulted in an unpleasant outcome, then it's likely that you have taught yourself to repress your emotions so that the same scenario doesn't play out again. Remember that you're only ever responsible for how you react. You're entitled to express your full range of emotions once you're not harmful or violent towards any other human being. Anger or frustration, for example, is not harmful if they are processed healthily with yourself or a therapist. They only become toxic when you don't learn to express your emotions as they arise. Bottled-up emotions will eventually spill out and become directed towards other people. Anger can cloud your mind and cause you to lash out if you're not in control. It's your responsibility to acknowledge the emotions that you have stored in your shadow self and to heal them so that this doesn't happen. There are plenty of ways that you can safely release your repressed emotions without taking them out on others or letting them run rampant in your life. As always, be kind to yourself as you go through this process, and praise yourself for taking the time to heal your repressed emotions. If the emotions are linked to childhood, take your inner child by the hand, and let them know that they are in a space where they will not be ridiculed or punished. It is now safe to express these emotions. A child who was told to stop crying will often believe that crying is considered weak and will never allow themselves to cry because of this. Allowing the floodgates to open can release years of pent-up tension and offer huge emotional relief. Crying is very beneficial to our health, and tears held in will often lead to headaches or other physical ailments. Let them go and start to let yourself heal. Begin working on your repressed emotions, and you find that a lot of sadness or anger comes up. Your automatic reaction may be to push it back down. Still, if you allow it to release in whatever way it needs to — by crying, shouting into a pillow, or writing it down. They can finally escape your unconscious mind and your body for good.

If you never had a safe space to express your emotions growing up, it could be helpful to seek one out now, possibly in the form of therapy. A therapist can help you name and understand your feelings and provide a safe space to express your feelings comfortably. According to an article on healthline.com, Emotionally Focused Therapy (EFT) may be especially beneficial for emotional repression. EFT emphasizes emotional expression to improve the way that you relate to yourself and others. It can help you work through childhood trauma, mental health issues and is even used in couples therapy (Raypole, 2020). Energy healing such as Reiki is also great for clearing repressed emotions. The Reiki practitioner will help you to balance your energy field by encouraging trapped emotions to come to the surface to be released. According to an article on reiki-waves.com, energy from repressed emotions is stored in the organs and tissues of the body. Reiki can help us release these emotions, resulting in deep healing (Sue, n.d.). Either one of these methods, or a combination of therapy and energy healing, might make resolving your repressed emotions a smoother process for you. It is always wise to accept help from people who understand what you're going through, especially those who also have the knowledge to help you. Love and support from a like-minded soul will always accelerate the healing process and make it easier. The most commonly repressed emotions are perceived as negative, such as fear, anger, sadness, and disappointment. Love and understanding are what will give those emotions the space they need to be expressed and released.

Here are some things you can try right now if you're eager to begin getting back in touch with those emotions that have been hidden deep in your unconscious mind.

1. Take a deep breath and check-in with yourself. What do you notice? Where are your thoughts racing to? Is there a negative thought or worry that is repeating? See if you can allow the emotion behind that thought to come forward and just sit with it. If you can't name the emotion yet, that's ok. The first step is allowing yourself to feel with no judgment. Breathe wherever you feel the tension in your body and tell yourself it's ok. If you feel sadness coming up, don't rush to push it down and think of something that makes you happy; allow the sadness to rise and accept it. Embrace it like you would a child who was sad and needed to express that emotion. Offer yourself love and give yourself time to feel whatever it is that you're feeling, right now in this present moment, without trying to change it. Remind yourself that you're doing just fine. If you start to feel anxious, you can use a breathing exercise to stay calm and allow the negative emotion to pass through you. The 4-7-8 technique is fantastic for calming the mind and body; it involves breathing in for four seconds, holding the breath for seven seconds, and exhaling for eight seconds (Fletcher, 2019).

2. Name your emotions. Practice naming any emotion you have as it comes up so that when repressed emotions come to the surface, you're in the habit of naming them and thus recognizing them. Sit still and notice how you feel for a moment. Can you name that emotion that you're feeling? Is it frustration? Anger? Sadness? See if you can name it without judging yourself for feeling that way. Accept how you feel and do nothing about it. Recognizing which emotion you're feeling

is an important step in allowing yourself to feel them and then resolve them.

3. Practice expressing your emotions with yourself and others. You can express your emotions with yourself in several ways. This could mean allowing yourself to feel what you're feeling with no judgment, naming the emotion, and releasing it verbally through crying or physically through exercise or movement. You may prefer to remove through writing, painting, or drawing. Whatever way you choose to express yourself is perfect and should be uniquely tailored to you. Journaling is an especially useful way to express your emotions privately. Writing down what you're feeling will help you to identify why you're feeling that way and how you can prevent those feelings from being pushed down and repressed in the future. Confiding in the person, you trust most in the world by sharing some feelings you have kept to yourself. Telling them about the shadow work you're doing can offer you emotional release and bring you closer to them in the process.

4. Whatever way you choose to resolve your repressed emotions, make sure that you continuously praise yourself for getting this far. It's very common for repressed emotions to be linked to the neglected inner child discussed in Chapter 2. Create a safe mental space for you and your inner child to resolve any repressed emotions you have been holding onto. Remember that it takes a brave soul to dig deep into their unconscious mind and pull out what lurks there. Once you do, you will heal yourself and improve your life in ways you could never have imagined. Well done for getting this far and investing in your future. You've got this.

FIVE

Identifying the Shadow Self

"Your Shadow is all of the things, 'positive' and 'negative,' that you've denied about yourself and hidden beneath the surface of the mask you forgot that you're wearing" (Anderson, 2016).

ARE YOU READY TO IDENTIFY YOUR SHADOW SELF? ALL YOU need to do is be willing to accept that we all have a shadow self that contains good and bad parts of ourselves. The intention is fundamental with shadow work. If you have the intention to consciously notice the shadow when it rises, then you will. When we think of the shadow self, we usually think of the more negative shadow aspects: fear, greed, sadness, and judgment. Then, there are also the positive aspects of our shadow self that we cannot see because of a limiting thought or belief blocking it. The unconscious mind will not allow us to see our potential because our self-esteem is too low or we do not believe in our abilities. Both the positive and negative sides of the shadow should be embraced equally. Just like there is no light without darkness, there is no negative shadow without the positive shadow. The balance of the two is what will make working on your shadow self so rewarding. You will be able to stop negative habits and patterns. Still, you will also discover hidden aspects of yourself.

Like abilities and talents that you never knew you had because you didn't have enough self-love to believe in yourself. That is why cultivating self-love, as we discussed in earlier chapters, is an essential part of this journey. Let's have a look at the difference between the positive shadow and the negative shadow and how they might appear in your life if you're ready to allow them into your consciousness. Again, the intent is all that matters. Once you intend to identify and embrace all aspects of your shadow self, you will find that you see your shadow self everywhere you look. Waiting for you to embrace it with your love and light. Embracing all aspects of your shadow self, whether you deem them positive or negative, is the doorway to finding your true self.

The Positive Shadow

Positive aspects of your shadow are hidden under a veil of low self-esteem, lack of confidence, and believing that you aren't good enough. These are limiting beliefs that you formed somewhere along the way as you were developing and reaffirmed for yourself time and time again, have become so ingrained in your thought process that it can be hard to identify positive aspects of your shadow at all. This thought process can be changed. Habits can be changed. We just have to be willing to put the work in. Everybody has hidden parts of their personality within their shadow self that could help them be more confident, creative, and happy. The trick is to notice ways in which you're afraid of your power. There can be many different reasons that you're fearful of your strength. Still, they all stem from fear — fear that you will be ridiculed for sharing your talents or fear that you don't fit in because your passions are different from the talents of the people around you. These fears can be debilitating to your growth, pushing those talents, gifts, and abilities into your shadow self so that they become an unconscious part of you that you don't have to address.

Let's look at an example of how somebody's talents can be repressed at a young age and how she can identify it as part of her positive shadow self as she grows older. We will call our little girl Anna. At eight years old, Anna started to write wonderful poetry. Every time that Anna wrote a poem, she felt amazing. She lost track of time and immersed herself in her words. Anna kept her poetry a secret, knowing that this is what makes her special, until one day, she decided to stay in the classroom at lunchtime instead of going out to play. She spent her lunch break writing beautiful poetry and her teacher later read it aloud to the class. The other children mocked Anna for her deep and thoughtful poetry. They were jealous that she was given attention and praise, and after school, they teased her. That is the point where Anna started to repress her talent for writing poetry. She started to perceive the fact that being unique was a negative thing. She stopped writing altogether in the hopes that she could fit in. Anna's talent was pushed deep into her unconscious mind to form part of her young shadow self. Fast forward 20 years, and Anna notices that her boyfriend has a job he loves, whereas she doesn't feel fulfilled. She is secretly jealous of him. The positive part of her shadow has negatively manifested itself. Her love for writing poetry has been so repressed that she is envious of anybody who can express their true self and embrace their talents. She feared ridicule and thought it was safer to avoid it at all costs, even if it meant feeling miserable.

This story shows how you can identify the positive aspects of your shadow self. We will discuss how to heal them later, but first, you must learn to identify them. You may not have a visible talent like writing or painting. It could be something more subtle, like a gift for working with animals or a strong intuition. Whatever your positive shadow self contains, an excellent place to start is to notice the qualities you admire about other people and wish you had yourself. The truth is, we cannot see anything in our outer world that does not exist in our inner world. Anything that you see in others is within you, too. If you know somebody who is living their life to the fullest and you can see that they're doing what makes them happy, take a look at the exact qualities you're noticing within them. Do they follow their gut instincts and end up exactly where they need to be, whereas you stress and worry and seem to get nowhere? That is an indication that you possess the same gift of strong intuition. Do you know somebody who is exceptionally witty and lightens up the room? At the same time, you overthink every word that comes out of your mouth? The chances are that if you question why you're envious of their wit, you will discover that you possess that same ability to make people laugh. Still, at some point in your life, you were told you were too loud or not funny enough, and so you repressed this part of yourself for fear of rejection.

All positive aspects of your shadow self are things within you that you were once led to believe are either too much or not enough, and so you decided to make yourself small. Doing this does not serve you well. To be your happiest self, you need to embrace all parts of yourself, especially the parts that make you different. Your power is the thing that makes you unique. It's the quality that makes you stand out in the crowd. Sometimes we are afraid of our power because we know we can shine brightly, and we are afraid that if we do, we might dim another person's light and be hated for it. This is a damaging belief. When you shine brighter and live authentically and truthfully, it encourages those around you to do the same. Surround yourself with people who are comfortable with who they are. Watch how they use their gifts and abilities to help them succeed. Try to hold onto the awareness that you wouldn't notice these people and their positive aspects if you didn't possess them too. Use that awareness to notice when a limiting belief about yourself comes up. Once you're conscious of watching out for the signs, you will see them. You're a perfect, unique human being, and you deserve to step into your power just like anybody else. Enjoy the journey of re-discovering the positive aspects of your personality that you have hidden. It may be painful at first to face the fear that kept them hidden. Still, the reward of stepping into your power and integrating your shadow so that you can live more freely is well worth it.

The Negative Shadow

Anything that you perceive as negative within yourself is not necessarily a negative trait. It's just your perception of it. You possess a full range of emotions, and as a human being, there is a time and place for every one of those emotions. You're entitled to feel every emotion within you, and you're entitled to think any thought that you have. Like everything in life, we need the things we perceive as negative to balance out what we perceive as positive. The parts of your shadow self that you might perceive as negative are emotions such as anger, sadness, or anxiousness. These things are valid and can help you move forward in your life if you can embrace them and accept them. Remember that these emotions became repressed and formed part of your shadow self only because you believed it was wrong to feel them. By repressing them, you can't express them at the right time, and they become misplaced, showing up as an overreaction that may cause pain and suffering for you and others. This cycle will continue, solidifying your belief that they are wrong until you can allow them to come into the light. This can show up in your life through addiction or depression. When you ignore parts of yourself and don't allow yourself to feel the full range of your emotions, you become unaware that those emotions are there at all. This can lead to you drinking your troubles away. You don't have to feel any emotions that you're uncomfortable with or feeling anxious and depressed without knowing why. There is always a perfect reason for any sort of addiction or struggle. The secret is to become conscious of it. When it is unconscious, it can drive your choices in life and cause unnecessary suffering. Suppose you're willing to identify the parts of your shadow self that you perceive as negative. In that case, you can integrate them into your personality and take away their power, thus taking away the need for the addiction.

An example of the negative shadow in a person's life would be a man told as a child that showing his emotions was weak. Let's call this man Jim. When Jim was five years old, his mother died. He didn't fully understand what this meant at the time, only that she was gone. He was sad and angry that his mother was no longer around, but he didn't know how to deal with this, so he would act out by misbehaving and crying when he didn't get what he wanted. Any time that he expressed his emotion, he was told to be quiet and stop crying. He was told that big boys don't cry. Jim formed a belief that feeling sad and angry was wrong. He eventually repressed these emotions, and they formed part of his shadow self, which he unconsciously labeled as negative. Now, when Jim feels sadness or anger, he pushes it down and tells himself that men don't show their emotions. He believes that to be strong, he needs to block out any negative emotions that make him appear weak, so Jim keeps all of his worries to himself. The first time Jim ever felt angry was when his mother died. As a child, he didn't realize what had happened. He thought that she had left him. Then, he was told that he was wrong to express his anger, and he carried that belief into his adult life.

This shows how all of us can identify hidden aspects of our shadow that we labeled as negative. Just like you can see the positive aspects of your shadow in others, the negative shadow is visible to us through others. What are the qualities in other people that make your blood boil? Try to become conscious enough to consider that perhaps you're so irritated by these qualities in others because you possess them somewhere in your unconscious mind, too, and the irritation comes from within yourself. This is not easy and will require a lot of introspection. Still, with love and understanding for the parts of yourself that you labeled negative long ago, you can learn to embrace them and allow them to serve their purpose at the right time and place. Once you make the unconscious parts of yourself conscious, you eliminate the need to run your life unconsciously and repeat the same old cycle, keeping you stuck. Embracing things you see as negative, and allowing them to take their rightful place in your life, will liberate you to live your life authentically because there is no part of yourself that you're rejecting.

SIX

How to Unveil the Shadow Self

"This thing of darkness, I acknowledge mine"
(Shakespeare & Kermode, 1998).

UNVEILING YOUR SHADOW SELF SO THAT YOU CAN EMBRACE your true nature and release your power is one of the best things that you can ever do for yourself. Like all healing, it's not going to be easy. Still, if you're interested in shadow work and have gotten this far, then you probably already know that. You're a warrior who can weather any storm and fight any demons that come your way, but here are a few tools that you can use to help unveil your shadow self. These tools will help you to embrace the good, the bad, and the ugly. Healing is messy. It's not all rainbows and butterflies, relaxing yoga, and deep breaths. It involves digging deep down into your soul and dragging out the parts of yourself that have always been hidden. When you learn to understand yourself, your consciousness expands. When your consciousness expands, you raise your awareness and then your vibration, leading to a more joyful and fulfilled life because you feel whole. You're no longer neglecting parts of your personality. So, you wonderful human being, let's have a look at some of the ways you can make the process easier for yourself. As always, when you use these tools to unveil your shadow self, please remember to be kind to yourself. Give yourself the love and space that you need to allow what you perceive as negative to come forward. You deserve it. You're well on your way to your best self.

Meditation

According to an article posted on verywellmind.com, meditation can be explained as a technique intended to encourage a heightened state of awareness and focused attention (Kendra Cherry, 2019). Meditating can seem daunting if you've never tried it before, especially if you have a racing mind. You may wonder how to sit still long enough to meditate. You may wonder how you can stop your thoughts from jumping from one thing to the next. The good news is that meditation can be personal to everybody. One way to enjoy meditation is utilizing guided meditation, where somebody speaks to you and guides your mind to where it needs to go. These are great for beginners, and there are plenty to be found online. Another option that you may enjoy is to meditate to soothing music. Some people also like to just sit in silence while they meditate. Whatever works for you is perfect. The main thing is that you're taking the time out of your day to expand your consciousness. So how does this help to unveil your shadow self? As you get in the habit of allowing yourself to be still, you will start to notice what repetitive emotions and thoughts pop up. The goal of meditation is to empty your mind of stress. When you find this particularly difficult to do, it is because your shadow self is trying to come through to your awareness to be healed. When something repeats in our mind every time we are quiet, it is a sign that it has been hidden in the shadows and needs to be dealt with.

Here is a short meditation that you can try, for just five minutes every day, that will help you to unveil your shadow self:

1. Find a quiet place to relax and get comfortable. You can lie down or stay seated with your legs crossed and your hands resting on your knees. You're welcome to play some soft, relaxing music.
2. Set a timer for five minutes and ensure that you will not be disturbed.
3. Close your eyes and inhale deeply. When you exhale, allow all of the stress to leave your body with the out-breath. Repeat this three times.
4. Start to become aware of your body. Is it warm or cold? What sensations can you feel? Where in your body do you feel tense? Breathe into that space.
5. As you are breathing and becoming aware of your body, you are being pulled into the present moment and raising your consciousness. While this happens, your shadow self will try to pull you back with thoughts and feelings about the past and future.
6. Notice if a thought is repeating in your mind. Are you thinking about what you need to do later? Are you feeling anxious about giving yourself this time? Do you feel sad or angry?
7. When you can see the thought process or emotion, just notice it and sit back and observe. Do not try to change it. Do not judge yourself. If you feel sad, let yourself cry. If you feel angry, let yourself feel that rage. Notice where you feel it in your body.
8. Lastly, repeat this affirmation to yourself: I am fully whole and perfect, just the way I am.

Your shadow self was born from a belief that you needed

to protect yourself from feeling certain emotions or expressing specific thoughts. Anytime that you meditate and become fully present, your shadow self will use this opportunity to pop up and remind you why you should constantly be on edge. Whether the underlying emotion is anger, grief, disappointment, or frustration, you're entitled to feel it. If you use this meditation regularly, you should start to see a pattern. When the same emotion or fear rises, again and again, it is a part of your shadow trying to overrule your thoughts. You have the power to allow yourself to feel the emotion, breathe, and embrace that part of yourself so that it can come out of the shadows and into the light. Meditate regularly for the best results.

Journaling

A fantastic way to unveil parts of your shadow self is through journaling. Journaling is great for your mental health and can help you clear your mind by spilling your thoughts onto the page and giving them a new home. If you can take the time to journal every day or once a week, you will start to notice patterns that pop up, just like with meditation. The key to all of these tools is to use them frequently. Repetitive thoughts and feelings will arise when you take the time to quiet your mind and allow them to come forward. Once they do, you immediately become conscious of them and embrace them into your light with love and acceptance.

Use this journaling exercise to help you unveil anything that has been hidden in your unconscious mind and formed as part of your shadow self, whether positive or negative. Journaling is one of the best ways to unveil the positive aspects of your shadow. As you write about what makes you happy, you start to uncover where you're holding yourself back. You may have gifts and talents that you have forgotten all about, waiting to be unveiled.

1. Make sure you're somewhere quiet and private. Set a couple of minutes aside for yourself when you will not be disturbed, and set a timer.
2. You can use a pen and a blank piece of paper, or a keyboard and a blank document on a computer.
3. Write this prompt at the top of the page: Today I feel…
4. Allow yourself to write until the timer has gone off. Don't stop to think about what you're writing, and don't worry about spelling mistakes or grammar. What you write doesn't even have to make sense. The idea is to get the words on the page. If you write the thoughts in your head down as they occur to you, you will be able to make sense of them later.
5. When the time is up, read back through what you have written. Does anything surprise you? Were you aware of how you were truly feeling before you wrote it down? If you wish, you can burn the paper when you're finished. This can be very therapeutic and remind you that this exercise is only for you.

Here are some other journaling prompts that you can use to unveil positive and negative qualities of your shadow self:

1. The trait I most admire in others is…
2. A trait I dislike in others is…
3. I feel weak when…
4. I feel powerful when…
5. If money weren't an option, I would…
6. If nobody would judge me, I would…
7. Three things I like about myself are…
8. Three things I dislike about myself are…

Therapy

Often, the thing that we need to accept ourselves is to see that other people accept us. This mirror provides us with the confidence to face the fear of rejection or failure that is holding us back. Therapy is a great way to do this for yourself while getting the help you need to tackle shadow work and become aware of the hidden aspects of your personality. A therapist will identify where you're causing unnecessary suffering for yourself, and they will help you heal it psychologically. If you're struggling with shadow work yourself, or even if you're not, therapy will provide you with that extra bit of support to make things a little easier. While your shadow self is a part of your unconscious mind, it's also a part of your energy field. It affects your mind, body, and soul since they are all connected. Combining therapy with a spiritual practice such as meditation would be a powerful way to unveil your shadow self. By looking at the same limiting belief or emotion from both spiritual and psychological perspectives, you will clearly understand the root cause and fully integrate them.

There are many forms of therapy that you can try, and most therapists will help you unveil your shadow self. A particular therapy that comes to mind is one that was created by therapist Marissa Peer. According to RTT.com's official website, RTT.com, Rapid Transformational Therapy (RTT) combines hypnotherapy, hypnosis, and regular therapy. The therapy aims to help you access, and communicate with, the unconscious parts of your mind. Doing this will uncover repressed memories and feelings and discover the interpretation and meaning you gave to that memory. Peer claims that you will only need one to three sessions to get to the root cause of your issue (Peer 2021). It makes sense that this would help unveil your shadow self. For example, suppose you were an only child for a long time, and your parents had another baby. In that case, you may have interpreted that as meaning that you weren't good enough. You may have felt like you were being replaced. When you relive this memory as an adult, you see that, of course, that wasn't the case, and your parents loved you so much that they didn't want you to be lonely, so they gave you a sibling. The meaning that you gave to this event as a child was stored as a repressed belief that you were not good enough and formed your shadow self. Diving into your unconscious mind in this way and reliving a memory to change your perception of it could be a compelling way to unveil and heal the shadow self very quickly.

Dreams

Another way that you can unveil parts of your shadow self is by paying attention to your dreams. Dreams are like hidden portals to our unconscious minds, and they can tell us a lot about what is hidden in the shadow. Sometimes, while we are doing shadow work through meditation, journaling, therapy, or other methods, shadow aspects of ourselves will come forward in dreams, hoping to be accepted and loved. If we miss these, we miss out on a huge opportunity to see behind the veil and understand what drives our unconscious mind. One of the most common dreams people have is that their teeth are falling out. This is a stress dream that is nudging us to notice that we are not aware of or not addressing stress in our life. Our dreams can be an ideal way to confront the unconscious parts of ourselves. According to an article on world-of-lucid-dreaming.com, dreams can directly reveal a physical manifestation of our shadow self through a dream character (Hammond, n.d.). Do you have a recurring dream that comes to mind? Is there a scary monster or villain that appears in your dreams from time to time? This is likely your shadow self. Sometimes these types of dreams contain a meaning that only you can decipher. Your shadow self may be trying to reach you through your dreams to show you precisely what is hidden there.

If you don't remember your dreams, don't worry. Here are some tips that will help you to remember your dreams so that you can try to understand the meaning of them and unveil your shadow self through your dreams:

1. Keep a dream journal or a pen and paper beside your bed. We do not remember every dream that we have, and often we have multiple dreams a night that get all jumbled up in each other. If you write down your dream immediately when you wake up, your brain will be more likely to remember them and find meaning. Plus, you can always revisit what you wrote later. Do this even if you wake up in the middle of the night to get into the habit of remembering your dreams.
2. Before you go to sleep, set an intention to remember your dreams. Your brain is more powerful than you know, and just setting this intention will help it remember an important dream.
3. Visualize your shadow self-visiting yourself in your dream. Imagine what you might say to it. If your fears manifest themselves in your dream as a man chasing you, maybe you could stop running? Could you turn around and face the dream man? Could you ask him what he wants? Suppose you visualize doing this a few times while you're awake. In that case, you will usually become conscious enough to do it while the dream is happening.
4. If you have had any recurring dreams that were very vivid throughout your life, they may be holding the key to an aspect of your shadow self. Write down everything you can remember about

this dream and how you felt while you were in it. This emotion is likely the one that you're repressing in your shadow.

All of the tools mentioned above can help you to unveil your shadow self. You must continue to work on embracing your inner child to get the most out of them. Your shadow self will not be revealed overnight, no matter how many tools you use. It will always reveal itself at the perfect time when you're ready to see it. All you can do is cultivate enough self-love that you're waiting with your arms open wide, full of acceptance for the darkest parts of your shadow self. Then, when the time is right, you will be ready to unveil it and heal it.

SEVEN

Understanding The Subconscious Mind

"As you sow in your subconscious mind, so shall you reap in your body and environment" (Murphy, 2019).

THE SUBCONSCIOUS MIND PLAYS A VITAL ROLE IN THE discovery of your shadow self. The unconscious mind and the subconscious mind can be easily confused, but think of it this way. The unconscious mind is where our shadow self is hidden along with our past traumatic experiences. The subconscious is our automatic reactions to different scenarios or situations based on those memories and experiences in our unconscious mind that we aren't aware of. If we think about it, we can usually link those reactions to the moment they were formed. For example, you might hate the smell of celery and feel sick even thinking about eating it. If you stop to wonder why, you might remember that your mother once made you eat celery when you were younger, even though you hated it. You threw the celery up, and now this memory is linked to your reaction to the vegetable. This is why the subconscious mind can be a beneficial way to access our shadow self. By becoming aware of the subconscious reactions we hold on to, we can become aware of unconscious habits and patterns within the shadow self.

The Role of the Mind

The subconscious mind is one of the most powerful inner sources that drive human nature because it guides all automatic movements. Do you remember when you learned to walk for the first time? Or when you learned to ride a bike or drive a car? These first attempts to learn a new skill and master a synchronized set of movements are usually difficult. We are conscious when we learn them. Over time, they require less and less conscious awareness until eventually, we do not even have to think about it anymore. That is the beauty of the subconscious mind. It is like an unlimited memory bank that permanently stores everything that ever happens to you. According to an article on briantracy.com, by the time you're 21, you've already permanently stored more than 100 times the contents of the entire Encyclopedia Britannica (Brian Tracy, 2018). The role of your subconscious mind is to store and retrieve data. It is responsible for regulating your body temperature and making sure you breathe. It also keeps your heart beating and works with your autonomic nervous system and the hundreds of chemicals in your cells to ensure that there is balance and harmony at all times.

Under hypnosis, people can often remember things such as memories that they had previously forgotten. The subconscious mind has perfect recall once we can access these memories. The thing is, the subconscious mind is a subjective slave to your conscious mind, which means that it will obey any command given by you consciously. This is another way that it differs from the unconscious shadow self. It is much easier to reprogram your subconscious mind than it is your unconscious mind. All you need to do is give it an order. That is why positive affirmations and meditation work for so many people. Affirmations and positive thoughts are stored in your subconscious. If you repeat them enough, they will start to form positive habits and reactions. The subconscious mind is your loyal servant and will follow your orders without bias. If you have a lot of negative self-talk going on, your subconscious will help you prove how useless you are. If you complain to others all day long, your subconscious mind will look for more reasons for you to complain.

On the other hand, if you practice positive self-talk and stop complaining, your mind will program itself to help you manifest the positive things that you keep thinking about and talking about. A subconscious mind is an excellent tool when used in the right way. It can help you reach your goals and manifest the life of your dreams; however, you must become conscious of how you're talking to yourself and others to achieve this. If you can form a positive thought pattern, it will override any negative pattern that your subconscious mind has created. All it takes is a little perseverance. Become conscious of any negative self-talk, and stop it immediately, replacing it with an affirmation that makes you feel good about yourself. You can start right now, at this very moment. The power lies within you.

Reprogramming the Mind

Because all of your habits, including how you talk, think, and practice, are stored in your subconscious mind. This means that all of your comfort zones are memorized. Your subconscious wants to protect you by making sure you continue to talk and think and act in the same manner that you always have to keep you safe, away from the unknown. This can be detrimental to your spiritual and mental growth, so it is important to reprogram your subconscious mind. The good news is you have complete control and the power to do so. All you need is a little bit of determination. So how do you go about reprogramming your subconscious mind? Well, anytime that you do something new that you can't predict the outcome to, your mind will give you a nudge in the form of fear. It produces feelings of anxiety and worry to protect you from making a mistake and ending up hurt. Once you notice those feelings, it is a sure sign that your subconscious mind has already been activated. Habits create patterns, and the secret to breaking the old ways of the subconscious mind is to develop new habits. It will not be easy to get out of your comfort zone without feeling uneasy, so you need to get comfortable with the uneasy feeling. Get comfortable with the uncomfortable, and command your subconscious mind to accept that new experiences can be exciting. When the feelings of unease rise as you attempt to make a new friend or try something you were always scared of doing, just allow it to be. Find the joy in the exhilarating feeling of not knowing what is going to happen next.

Understand that your subconscious mind is keeping you safe, but it is also not allowing you to grow, and that the only way to grow is to get out of your comfort zone. See if you can enjoy stepping into the unknown and trying new things. Create healthy habits such as using daily affirmations in the morning to trick your subconscious brain into focusing on these new habits instead of the old ones. Remember that you are in complete control. Once you no longer fear the unknown, your subconscious has no hold on you. If you take steps to reprogram your mind to expand on your experiences, that will raise your conscious awareness. It will help you work on your shadow self and bring even more of your personality into the light. Go you!

Here are a couple of things that will help you to get started on reprogramming your mind:

1. Visualize your dream life. Gain a clear understanding of what your dream life would look like, and then try to identify the differences between the version of you in your visualization and the version of you today. What subconscious habits are getting in the way and keeping you comfortable instead of reaching for your dreams?
2. Commit to doing the work. Once you have decided what you want to change, keep a notepad and pen handy at all times. Any time that you hear negative chatter in your brain write it down. Whenever you catch yourself saying 'I can't' in your head or conversation, stop. Is this really what you want to tell your subconscious mind? Every time you catch it, replace it with I can.
3. Change your beliefs. Focus on positive self-talk and positive conversation with others. Use 'I am' affirmations daily. Repeat phrases such as 'I am perfect, just the way I am.' or 'I am fully deserving of a loving and happy relationship.' These affirmations will rewire your subconscious brain and replace outdated beliefs that no longer serve you with healthy new ones.

Like we've previously discussed, intention and self-love are essential for any self-work. Learn to develop a healthy relationship with yourself and your subconscious mind. For years you repeated the same habits and stayed within your comfort zone because your mind kept you safe. It's ok if you still feel scared. New beginnings scare everybody. The point is to embrace the fear rather than continuing to stay in your comfort zone. It is time for a new adventure, my friend.

EIGHT

The Shadow Self and Projection

"If you were easier on yourself, you wouldn't be so tough on everyone else" (Mcgahan, 2015).

THE SHADOW SELF AND PROJECTION ARE INTRICATELY LINKED. That is because when we externalize our unconscious thoughts, feelings, and beliefs and project them onto the world, it is the shadow self that we are projecting. When you're not conscious of your shadow self, you will not be conscious of how you're projecting it. Looking at projection can be a significant help on the journey to healing the shadow.

What Is Projection?

According to counselor and health and fitness writer Sara Lindberg, projection refers to unconsciously taking unwanted emotions or traits that you don't like about yourself and attributing them to someone else (Lindberg, 2018). A prevalent example is an unfaithful partner. Have you ever wondered why somebody cheating on their partner may become paranoid and suspect their faithful spouse of cheating? This is projection. Instead of acknowledging their infidelity, they are projecting their guilt onto their partner. This is essentially a self-defense mechanism that enables people to stay unconscious and blame the world for their problems. Of course, when somebody is projecting, they are entirely unaware of it since it is unconscious behavior. This behavior may protect you from facing aspects of yourself that you don't like. However, you will still see those traits in other people, so you aren't escaping them completely. It may be easier to see things you dislike in others rather than in yourself, but it doesn't ever solve the problem, does it? It keeps discomfort at bay, but it also keeps you separate from parts of yourself. As long as it stays unconscious, it won't be healed. That is why conscious awareness is needed to understand what projection is to notice it and then stop yourself when you do it. People prone to project are those with low self-esteem who don't believe that they're good enough, which is where a lot of the shadow self was likely formed. If you can learn to accept and love yourself, you will not need to project because you will be comfortable with who you are. Most of us project our personalities onto others in one way or another. The universe reflects what we are thinking and feeling. This is just the unconscious mind and the shadow self doing its job. Projection is a symptom of the shadow self. You may not like to hear that the things you don't like about other people are traits you possess, but it is true. Once you become aware of this, you can change your negative perception of this trait, learning to accept it within yourself and accept it within others. This will help you to bring the traits you're projecting out of the shadows for good. Don't worry. It is easy to spot when you're projecting once you're looking out for it.

How to Identify Projection

Identifying projection can be hard at first because our unconscious mind doesn't want us to acknowledge that we are doing it. Often, projection is happening because we are victimizing ourselves and haven't set healthy boundaries. We blame other people for something that we need to address ourselves. An example of projection would be insisting that somebody hates you, even though you have no evidence of this. The question to ask yourself is: Do I hate myself? Turning it back around on yourself will give you a clue as to whether your thinking or feeling is true about the other person. The reality is that when we are happy with who we are and we have set emotional boundaries for ourselves, other people's opinions of us don't matter so much. Your emotional reactions to things will not be so heightened if you have a healthy relationship with yourself. If somebody has upset you enough that it ruins your whole day, that could be a sign that you're projecting. You have the power to react in any way that you wish, and so does everybody else. You are not responsible for anybody else's reactions. When we know this, it becomes clear that any time somebody makes us feel intense emotions such as anger, disappointment, fear, or shame, there is a good chance that we have projected onto them. If your spouse asks you what you did for the day, and you become defensive and annoyed, assuming that he is interrogating you, maybe you're projecting your feelings of insecurity and low self-worth onto him. Your spouse may be simply curious about your day and trying to start a conversation. Still, if you're unconsciously telling yourself that you're not good enough and you need to do more with your day, then you will assume he thinks that too.

Here is a three-step process that you can use to identify when you're projecting:

Step 1: Notice anytime you feel hurt and defensive after an interaction with somebody. Did you let them get under your skin? Did you react too quickly and immediately blame them without listening? Do you find it hard to see things from the other person's point of view?

Step 2: Be honest with yourself. In what ways do you act like this person? Is this person triggering your past? Could you have misconstrued what they were saying to you?

Step 3: Implement boundaries for yourself. Whenever you feel overwhelmed, see if you can spend time self-reflecting rather than reacting to the person straight away. Set a boundary with them that you need time to yourself. During this time, explore what came up in step two. If you have been projecting, offer acceptance to the traits that irritated you when you saw them in another person. Remember that nobody is perfect.

How to Stop Projection

When you identify that you're projecting, note whether you have ever been in a similar situation before. Often, we repeat projection patterns because there is a deeply rooted issue that we don't want to address. See if you can find any patterns. Do you project only with romantic partners? Maybe you do it with your parents? Or perhaps you're finding ways that you do it with everyone? Seeing a pattern will help to figure out the reasoning behind your projecting. For example, suppose you project onto your parents that they are not proud of you. In that case, this could indicate that you're storing a belief from childhood in your unconscious mind. A belief that you're not good enough may cause you to project on many different people and situations when in fact, it is you who is not proud of yourself.

Remember, if you believe that you're not good enough,

your shadow self will look for ways to show you that you're right and reflect that belief to you. Catching projection as it happens can open the door to your shadow self and allow that belief to heal so that the projection and the pattern stops. Projection can skew your view of reality. It may seem like your boss is never happy with anything that you do, but what if it is you who is never proud of your work? Spending more time alone with your thoughts can help decipher what you're projecting and help you stop doing it. Question your beliefs regularly. The next time you think about how somebody in your life is hard on you, ask yourself if perhaps you're projecting this on to them because you do not want to deal with the fact that you're so hard on yourself?

Meditation and journaling can help stop projection because they encourage you to be more in touch with yourself and fully accept yourself. Just like self-love will allow your shadow self to come to light and be embraced, it will heal it from projecting, too. Be more compassionate towards yourself, and allow yourself to feel your full range of emotions. The next time that somebody asks you how you are stop to think about it. People get in the habit of saying, "I'm fine," even when they are falling apart. See if you can stop this habit immediately, and start being honest with yourself and others about how you're feeling. If you can acknowledge how you feel and be kind to yourself about what you don't like, there will be no need for projection anymore. Projection is just another defense mechanism that your unconscious mind is using to protect you. Remind yourself that you don't need protection anymore. Tell yourself that you have acquired the knowledge you need, and you're strong enough to take control. Believe in your ability to face your shadow self and embrace the things you don't like about yourself, and you will stop projecting in no time. You can handle it, you wonderful human being!

NINE

Facing Your Shadow Self

"You don't find the light by avoiding the darkness" (S Kelley Harrell & Pratt, 2004).

YOUR SHADOW SELF IS THE PLACE WHERE THE DARKEST SIDE OF your personality lives. It's where you need to go to face your darkness and accept it as part of you rather than trying to reject it. We all have a dark side, and that is not a bad thing. It is just the way the universe works. Good vs. evil, light vs. darkness, your light vs. your shadow self. This doesn't necessarily have to be the battle that you may imagine it to be. Facing your fears is the key to understanding that nothing is quite as scary as it seems in your mind, and once you face your shadow self, you will see that there was never anything to be scared of. There are qualities within your shadow self that will be helpful to you in your life. The aim is to embrace and understand your shadow, not to eliminate it from your psyche altogether. The darkness that you imagine is part of you exists alongside your light and has a purpose. Now that you're starting to understand what that purpose is, you're ready to face your shadow self by becoming consciously aware the next time you feel triggered. Your emotional triggers will make you aware of what is going on within your shadow self. Are you ready to learn how to heal your emotional triggers? This chapter is designed to help you spot your triggers and heal them to raise your consciousness and become more self-aware.

What Are Triggers?

A trigger is something that causes an emotional reaction within you. It could be a memory, an experience, or an event. A trigger sparks a particular emotional response within you regardless of your current mood. When you're triggered by something somebody says, the emotional reaction will be instantaneous. You will react before you have time to process how you're feeling. This is because triggers are usually linked to some sort of traumatic experience you had in the past. You're now reacting with your subconscious, reliving the trauma. Every time you relive that trauma by hearing a song that reminds you of it or watching somebody else go through a similar thing, your attachment to the trigger grows stronger. You may not be aware that your subconscious mind is creating this habit. Still, you will be aware of sudden and overwhelming emotions. For example, if you were criticized a lot by your parents as a child, your trigger would be feeling criticized. You may react emotionally to any feedback that is not entirely positive and cannot accept constructive criticism. If your partner suggests a change in your behavior, you may feel triggered and become defensive or upset. You need to become aware of your triggers and heal them because your shadow self remembers how painful it was the first time you were criticized, but you don't. You will keep replaying the original trauma each time you feel triggered and adding to your shadow self until you receive the love and understanding you need. Don't worry, though. You have the power to stop this cycle.

Identifying Emotional Triggers

Emotional triggers will be different for each person because we all have our own experiences, memories, and traumas. Some common situations can be emotional triggers for people, such as violence, betrayal, or rejection. Suppose you have ever been betrayed, and you haven't fully healed from the situation. In that case, there is a good chance that you will be triggered anytime that you suspect somebody might betray you. It's very common to feel physical symptoms when triggered, such as anxiety, heart palpitations, or trembling. If your mind replays an event, your body isn't aware that it's not happening now. It will respond in the same way it would if you were back in that situation. If you cried anytime your parents criticized you, you might start to cry whenever you feel criticized as an adult. Suppose you were trembling with anger when you were betrayed by your first boyfriend. In that case, you might start to shake anytime you even suspect betrayal now.

So how can you identify what your emotional triggers are? Find five minutes to yourself and sit down in a quiet space with a blank piece of paper. See if you can answer the following questions. They will help you to figure it out.

1. Have you noticed a topic of conversation that bothers you? If so, you might be triggered by this topic. For example, if hearing people making fun of others upsets you and reminds you of a time you were bullied, this is a trigger.
2. Do you feel envious when somebody shares their good news with you? If you do, you may be triggered by this topic because it's something that

you believe you can't have. If hearing about somebody's happy relationship upsets you and makes you feel sad to be single, this is a trigger stemming from a lack of self-love.

After answering the questions above, you should have a good understanding of how to spot a trigger. The next time that you notice yourself feeling emotionally triggered, just allow the emotions to arise, accept them, and then write them down when you're alone. Writing down how you felt will help you to understand what it was that triggered you and why. Once you can identify the root cause, you're ready to heal that trigger within your shadow self.

Healing Emotional Triggers

When people are triggered by outside events, they can either withdraw and avoid the emotion they are feeling or react by lashing out and causing more pain. Your emotional triggers are wounds that need to be healed. The thing to remember is that these triggers were likely formed when you were a child. They are built on outdated beliefs and no longer serve you because the fear caused you to develop an emotional trigger that may not be relevant to your adult life. The intense reaction you experience every time you're faced with triggers that fear is unnecessary, and it can be healed. To start the healing process, it's wise to look inward to try spotting any beliefs that you have formed. You must be gentle with yourself throughout this process. The reason you're triggered is that you're defending against a painful memory. Be kind to yourself and compassionately address your self-doubt. Whenever you notice that something has triggered you, try to see it from your inner child's perspective.

You may feel guilty for overreacting when a friend cancels a date with you, but if you think of a time that you felt abandoned as a child, you will see that your reaction is valid based on that event. Suppose your father made promises to attend school plays or football games but always ended up canceling. In that case, that is a very valid reason to fear people canceling on you. As a child, you may have believed that this meant you were not worthy of your father's time and attention. You then formed a belief that you're not good enough. Remember that this belief was formed from the perspective of a child. You had no understanding of the pressures your father might have been facing from work or anything else outside your perspective. You weren't able to identify that. Of course, you are good enough, and somebody being too busy to see you does not mean you are unworthy. If you can look through the eyes of your inner child the next time a friend cancels on you, you can start to heal the trigger. Soothe the part of you that is terrified and shouting 'I'm not good enough!' by offering yourself some love and understanding.

Once you've made yourself aware of your emotional triggers, you have taken the hardest step. Healing will come naturally once you start to understand how you might have formed a fear in the past that is not necessary to have now. Some fears are created later in life, too, of course. You may have formed a fear of abandonment as a teenager when you experienced your first heartbreak. Perhaps you fought and broke up. This can cause arguments to be the emotional trigger for your fear of abandonment. You may fear that somebody will abandon you any time that you disagree with them. Understand that emotional triggers are always about your unconscious mind reliving a past event. Remind yourself that you're safe, and if the same thing did happen again, you would be just fine because you're stronger now than the first time it happened. In the meantime, free yourself from unnecessary suffering by reliving the same thing over and over. Heal your emotional triggers by bringing them into the light and facing them head-on. Look at your fears and see if they are as scary as you thought. Would you survive if your worst fear materialized? The likelihood is that you would. You're far more resilient than your shadow self thinks you are. The only way to teach it is to become aware that it shows you what needs to be healed and offer it love and acceptance instead of giving in to the fear. As always, love is the thing that will heal you. Love, in the face of fear, will triumph. So off you go, brave one. Go slay your emotional dragons and heal your triggers. Visualize so that you can free yourself. Once you free yourself from emotional triggers, there is a new level of emotional intelligence and a new level of awareness waiting on the other side.

TEN

Healing Shadow Wounds

"Our wounds are often the openings into the best and most beautiful parts of us" (Richo, 2014).

YOU KNOW BY NOW THAT YOUR SHADOW SELF WAS FORMED when you were a child. It's common for the shadow to form at the first moment that your needs are not being met by your caregivers. The trauma that caused you to feel neglected could have been an actual traumatic event such as abuse or the death of a loved one, or the trauma could be a rupture in the way you see the world. Whatever it was that caused your shadow self to be born, the wound is equally as painful. That pain is the key to healing your deepest shadow wounds. The scars that have been there the longest are your inner child's trauma. The emotional pain that occurs when our inner child's wound is triggered and we relive the trauma is a part of that wound that needs to be healed in its own right. Let's look at how you can start to work with your inner child to heal your past trauma and how you can work with your adult self to heal emotional pain that is more recent. Take a deep breath and remember to feel gratitude for being here at this moment. You have gained the self-awareness to get this far. You have taken responsibility for your pain and chosen to heal it so that you don't project it onto others and cause more pain. You're choosing a life full of free will and conscious thought. Once you have given yourself a big hug, it's time to take your inner child by the hand and tread gently through the landscape of the trauma that made them feel neglected. You're one step closer to a new level of self-awareness.

Healing Your Inner Child's Trauma

All trauma that we hold on to as a child is a result of misplaced blame and guilt. When our ability to safely be ourselves is threatened, and we have to reach a new understanding of the world around us, we think it's our fault. We feel guilty for not being able to figure out how to fix everything. Your neglected inner child is the one that you will need to work with to get to the root of this trauma. Do you remember the story of the little girl who loved to write in Chapter 2? She first felt neglected when she lost the ability to do the only thing that helped her escape the pain of being bullied. The writing was her escape, but she gave up her gift and buried it in her shadow self to fit in. She could never communicate properly when she grew up until she discovered this hidden part of her and reconnected with it. Writing as an adult set her free. This is how your story is going to go. Whatever caused your inner child to feel neglected, you can journey back to that moment and see it from a different perspective now. You're older and wiser now, and once you keep an open mind and an open heart, you will be able to heal whatever your trauma is too. In that little girl's case, her inner child's trauma type was neglect due to the ridicule and teasing she faced when she shared her gift.

Let's take a look at four types of inner child wounds, how they might show up in your life:

1. **Abandonment:** You find it hard to be alone. You attract emotionally unavailable people, and being left out is a huge trigger for you.

2. **Neglect:** You struggle with low self-worth and find it hard to say no. You can't let go of the past. You find it hard to connect emotionally with people, and heightened emotions trigger you.

3. **Guilt:** You say sorry a lot and don't like asking for help. You attract people who make you feel guilty, and criticism triggers you.

4. **Trust:** You find it hard to trust other people and even yourself. You're scared of being hurt and need constant validation. You attract people who do not make you feel safe, and people breaking promises triggers you.

Now, let's have a look at how you can heal these wounds. You have been attracting people and situations that validate these wounds for you, but you have the power to stop this cycle of pain. First, take a moment to meditate and connect with your inner child. Close your eyes and visualize yourself as a child feeling one of these emotions. What age are you? Take deep breaths as you allow yourself to see the memory from a new perspective. The adult version of you is going to change the narrative. Be the adult that you needed to protect you or reassure you at that moment. Imagine sending love and acceptance to your younger self and telling them they are perfect just the way they are.

Here are some actions you can take that will make

your inner child feel safe so that you can let go of the trauma:

1. **Abandonment:** Spend time alone, and retreat into yourself for a while, allowing your inner child to show you the trauma that has been associated with this fear. The key is to prove to yourself that you're capable of being alone so that you can let the fear of abandonment go.

2. **Neglect:** Write your emotions down or go to therapy and share them. Set boundaries with others by learning to say no. Put yourself first. The key to healing feelings neglected by others is to first stop ignoring yourself.

3. **Guilt:** Accept help from others rather than carrying everything on your shoulders and feeling guilty for being overwhelmed. Self-love will help you to accept that nobody is perfect. The key is to become aware of when you're blaming yourself for things outside of your control, and remember you're striving to be your best self, which is something to be proud of.

4. **Trust:** Learn to trust yourself first. Meditation and journaling will help you to connect with your intuition. Your body tells you what is going on. Usually, when a trust wound is activated, we feel anxious and scared. The key is to catch the limiting beliefs that caused this wound. If you believe that somebody doing one thing and saying another means that they will hurt you, you need to face that belief and challenge it. Replace 'I can't trust anybody' with 'most people are trustworthy.'

Healing Emotional Pain

Healing emotional pain is achieved by being present with yourself and addressing the pain that you're holding onto right now. This is different from healing your inner child's traumas, where the goal is to find the source of the pain. To heal emotional pain, you do not necessarily need to know where the pain came from. You just need to choose to let go of your current pain and suffering by replacing it with self-love at this moment. The emotional pain you feel resulting from the core wounds you formed as a child will automatically ease when you work with the inner child. Understand that all that is happening is your shadow self has created this wound, and now it needs to validate the emotion the wound brings up in you. If your core wound is trust issues, you may have a pattern of attracting untrustworthy partners who validate that belief and show you that you're right to have trust issues. This cycle only stops when we address the core wound. Remember how we discussed that your shadow self can run your life on autopilot if you're unaware of it? This is a perfect example. The universal law of attraction will ensure that you attract what is within you. Your external world will mirror your inner world. Suppose your internal world is full of unconscious fears and traumas. In that case, your external world will be full of fears and traumas, and you won't stop experiencing them until you face what caused that pattern in the first place. While you're working with your inner child and healing core wounds, be aware of how these cycles play out in your adult life. Understanding that you're reliving the same memory over and over again in different ways is causing unnecessary suffering. Unfortunately, pain is necessary. As human beings, it's a pain that helps us grow; however, suffering is unnecessary. The beauty of this is that when you know where to look, your shadow self shows you precisely what you have hidden there. You will have to face the emotional pain connected to your trauma one more time to heal it and release it. Still, you won't continue to suffer by experiencing the same pain again through different situations.

When you notice a pattern, such as a history of unfaithful partners, you can do the best thing for your emotional pain to embrace it. Do the exact thing that your shadow self has been preventing you from doing. Choose to be alone. Choose to love yourself and sit with the pain. Journey back to the first time that you felt abandoned. It may have been your mother, father, or friend who wasn't there when you needed them. How did that make you feel? If you feel angry or sad, let those emotions rise. If it made you feel like you weren't good enough, that's ok. Let it in and feel it with every ounce of your being, and do whatever you need to do to let it out of your body. You have the power to release this fear that has been trapped inside your psyche and your body for so long. You deserve to let it go so that it does not need to live in your shadow self anymore. Creating scenarios where you feel abandoned and attracting people who will abandon you. You might even discover that you have left yourself at some point along the way by ignoring a gift that you had or denying yourself the freedom to pursue the career of your dreams. Accept all of this and forgive yourself. If you had known better, you would have done better. You're stronger now.

Notice where the fear lives in your body and tell it to leave. Allow it to pass through you and relive those emotions one more time BUT from the perspective of your adult self now. You will find that while your fear of abandonment was valid, it was not completely true. Your mother was not showing up when you needed her never meant that she didn't love you, and it certainly never meant that you weren't good enough. Be there for yourself as you process the emotions and let your childhood trauma rise to the surface. Give yourself whatever you need to feel better so that you come out of your little bubble and rejoin the world. There is no longer any need for these traumas to manifest themselves in your life. You're aware of them now, and that means your shadow self has done its job of showing you what you need to heal. Trust that you will see the triggers and notice when you're projecting. You have all the information that you need now to face and heal your shadow self. Well done for taking this challenging but rewarding journey. The exercises in the next chapter are designed for you to come back to time and time again whenever you need to work with your shadow self. You have got everything that you need within you.

ELEVEN

Shadow Work Exercises

"The mind is just like a muscle — the more you exercise it, the stronger it gets and the more it can expand" (Idowu Koyenikan, 2016).

According to Dr. Maxwell Maltz, it takes a minimum of 21 days to form a habit. His studies showed that this is because it takes this long for an old mental image to dissolve and a new one to set in (Maltz & Powers, 2010b). Because shadow work involves dissolving old thought patterns and beliefs and embracing new healthy ones, it would be a good idea to follow this line of thinking. Use one or all of these exercises every day for a minimum of 21 days to gain the most benefit from them. It can be helpful to choose to do the exercises simultaneously every day for consistency, but do what makes the most sense for you to seamlessly add these practices into your current lifestyle. Ease yourself into these exercises with mindfulness and gratitude, and remember to embrace your shadow self with love and acceptance. As you continue to do these exercises day after day, you will notice different memories and feelings come up that need to be healed. Every time you will go a little deeper and discover new shadow wounds so that you can coax them into the light.

Meditation

1. Find a quiet space to relax and get into a comfortable position, either lying down or your legs crossed and your hands resting on your knees. Face your palms up so that your hands are open and set the intention to receive the wisdom and clarity you're seeking. The answers are all within you.

2. Close your eyes and take a deep breath. Feel where there is tension in your body and breathe into it. Hold your breath for a few seconds, then breathe out, picturing the stress and tension leaving your body.

3. Picture a beautiful white light entering through the top of your head and making its way down your body, cleansing each chakra as it goes. Let it form a bubble around your body. This white light is your connection to source energy, and it will protect you while you connect with your shadow self. Remember, you are loved. You are safe. You are surrounded by white light.

4. Visualize your neglected inner child. See them reaching out to you and asking for love. Invite them into your bubble of white light. Give them what they need. If you don't know what they need, just sit in your white light and picture your inner child there with you. Wait for them to come forward and tell you what they are missing. You will know this unconsciously, but it may take a few minutes to become conscious of it. If you're struggling with this, choose something that you were lacking as a child. If you were bullied, offer your inner

child a friend. If you experienced neglect from a parent, offer them a supportive parent.

5. Allow your inner child to come forward and express their emotions. Remember that your inner child is you, so it's natural for you to feel uncomfortable emotions arise within you at this point. It's time to allow yourself to express the feelings that you couldn't as a child. You may feel anger, disappointment, sadness, or fear. Whatever you feel, keep soothing yourself and reminding yourself that you're a fully grown adult now. You can handle it. It's only a memory. All you need to do is let those emotions escape.

6. As you embrace the uncomfortable emotions that are rising, stay conscious that your shadow self will want to hold on to those negative emotions. The memory of being neglected brings up strong emotions, but it does not mean you're not good enough. Rationalize with your inner child, and teach them that nothing anybody else does is a reflection of who they are. Remember that you are loved, safe and do not need to bury your true feelings any longer.

7. Visualize the emotions, feelings, or beliefs that your inner child has formed and has held on to for so long. Picture these as grey shadows. Gently allow those feelings and memories to be absorbed by the white light that still surrounds you. Accept that you were right to feel that emotion at the time, and let go of any judgment towards yourself for feeling it. Let it go into the light. Allow the anger, fear, or sadness to fade into the light and be transmuted into love.

8. Visualize your inner child starting to smile and look and feel lighter. Let them release their burden and become childlike again. Picture them playing and laughing, feeling free.

9. Thank your inner child for working with you. Give them a big hug, and let them know that they do not need to be frightened anymore because you're there for them. You're there for yourself. You have faced your shadow self, and you survived.

10. Set an intention to keep your white light around you for the rest of the day.

11. When you open your eyes, notice how you feel. It may help to journal about the emotions that came up. Wrap your arms around yourself and feel gratitude for connecting with yourself and facing the darkest parts of yourself.

Mirroring

Mirror work involves using what people mirror back to you in your daily life to understand yourself better and unveil parts of your shadow self so that you can heal it. The mirror exercise will show you exactly what it is within your shadow self that is causing discomfort. This exercise can be done anytime, anywhere. It can help to write it down the first couple of times you use it. This is an excellent exercise to use as soon as you spot projection happening. It's also extremely helpful for gaining clarity whenever you feel triggered.

1. Picture a person who has annoyed you. What is it about them that got under your skin? Was it something they said or did?
2. Identify the personality trait that bothers you.
3. See if you can identify ways in which this trait exists in you.
4. Think about how this personality trait that you perceive as negative might be a strength. For example, if someone is stubborn, maybe this helps them to see tasks through to completion?
5. Ask yourself what you need to acknowledge and accept

about yourself for this trait to be balanced and come out of the shadows.

6. Decide an action and commit to it. Do you need to feel gratitude for your stubbornness and the positives it brings? Then list the ways it has helped you in the past, and praise yourself for being reliable.

Inner Dialogue

Your inner dialogue is the voice inside your head that is constantly narrating your life. You may be conscious of this, or you may not. To integrate your shadow self, you must start to become aware of your inner dialogue and how your shadow self is driving it. The unconscious mind is formed at a young age. Usually, our inner dialogue will echo the dialogue of our caregivers in our younger years. This is fine if your parents were loving and supportive. They taught you right from wrong and the basics of how to survive, of course. Still, suppose your parents were very critical of you. In that case, the chances are that you have adopted that critical voice as your inner dialogue. Think back to around the time your shadow self was formed. What were the people around you saying to you back then? Were you told you nothing you did was good enough? Were you told to stop crying and toughen up? The outer dialogue we hear in early life can influence the inner dialogue that we adopt hugely. Just like all parts of the subconscious mind, your inner dialogue likes to repeat patterns. Suppose your shadow self influences your inner dialogue. In that case, it will run on a loop and repeat the same thing repeatedly. You do have the power to change your inner dialogue and control your thoughts. It's part of becoming conscious of who you are. Do you know what your inner dialogue is telling you?

This exercise will help you identify what traits within your shadow self have caused a negative inner dialogue in your daily life. It will help you heal them. Thoughts tend to have a snowball effect — one bad thought will lead to another, and before you know it, you're having a terrible day. The key is to catch the bad thought before it ruins your mood and consciously choose a positive one instead.

1. Keep a notepad with you at all times for the next 21 days, and get into the habit of writing down any time that you notice you're speaking to yourself negatively. Any time you tell yourself, "I'm not good enough" or "I'm stupid" or "I can't do that," take note of it and immediately. You will start to see a pattern forming.

2. Look at the words on the page and ask yourself if you would say those words to somebody you love.

3. Now ask yourself why you're talking to yourself in a way that you wouldn't talk to somebody else.

4. See if you can identify the fearful belief that has created the thought that keeps repeating itself. Why do you believe you're not good enough? Did somebody tell you that long ago, and you decided it was a fact?

5. Replace it with an affirmation that negates that thought. For example, if your inner dialogue tells you that you're not good enough, replace that with an affirmation such as, "I am perfect and whole just the way I am."

6. Choose one thing you're grateful for about yourself and write that down too. Pick a good trait that you're proud of. Gratitude is very powerful. It can help you control your thoughts and steer them in a positive direction whenever you feel a negative inner dialogue pop up.

Journaling

There are many different uses for journaling when it comes to shadow work. You can use it to unveil your shadow self, as discussed in Chapter 6, or you can use it to keep track of your emotional triggers and repressed emotions. Below, you will find another journaling prompt that will help you connect with your inner child and heal a deep shadow wound. Working with your inner child will help you find the love and compassion you need to embrace your shadow after unveiling it. You deserve to feel good, especially when doing challenging shadow work, so enjoy this exercise. Use it as an opportunity to say all of the nice things to yourself that you wish you had heard from others when you were young.

Take a pen and a piece of paper for this one. Writing by hand will force your brain to engage with the words you're writing and remember them later. You're going to write a letter to your inner child. Visualize your younger self and pick an age that was difficult for you. Think back to a time that you needed reassurance from an adult but didn't get it. You're going to go back in time and offer yourself this reassurance now.

1. At the top of the page, write 'Dear Me.'
2. Conjure a clear image of yourself at the age you have chosen. What do you look like? Are you a happy child? Are you sad? Do you share your emotions with your caregivers or keep them bottled up?
3. When you have a clear image in your head, set a timer for 10 minutes.
4. During these 10 minutes, you must write whatever pops into your mind. Do not agonize over the words you write, spelling mistakes, or what your handwriting looks like. The only important thing is reassuring your younger self that everything is going to be ok. Tell them about your life now if you can't

think of anything else to say. This letter is from 'you' to 'you' so it doesn't have to be perfect.

5. Keep writing until the timer goes off. Even if you don't think you have much to say to your inner child, you will be surprised how your brain will spill your emotions onto the page when you just keep writing whatever pops into your head.

6. Read the letter back to yourself. If you can read it aloud, even better.

7. Notice any emotions that arise and be present with them. You may need to release some fear or sadness. See if you can feel gratitude for being able to be there for yourself, even if nobody else was.

8. Give yourself a big hug and visualize your inner child radiating love and happiness. Imagine them feeling loved and protected, knowing that everything is going to work out for the best.

Affirmations

Consistency is key for affirmations. They must be repeated frequently to sink into our subconscious minds. You can use affirmations to replace the subconscious negative thought that your shadow self has spent years working on with a conscious positive thought. Remember how your subconscious mind will do whatever you say? Well, if you say a positive affirmation often enough and for long enough, it will start to believe it to be true.

Be patient with yourself. It will take time, but it's worth it. Soon the part of your shadow that believes you aren't good enough and creates negative self-talk will have no choice but to accept that you're perfect just the way you are.

Choose one of these affirmations to work with each week. Be patient with yourself as you do this work.

1. I fully accept all of my unique gifts and talents.
2. I choose to love all parts of myself, exactly as I am.
3. I see love and abundance all around me, everywhere I go.
4. I am feeling more and more confident each and every day.
5. I have everything within me that I need to heal myself.
6. I am always worthy of love and happiness, just because I exist.
7. I see the beauty in others that exists in myself.
8. I am happy and healthy in mind, body, and spirit.

Tips: Write the affirmation down and place it on your desk or somewhere you will notice it regularly throughout your day. You could also record yourself saying the affirmation out loud and replay it every couple of hours.

TWELVE

Nurturing the Inner Child

> *"Behold the children and imitate them... They are interested in the present moment, in being curious and in learning, in showing and in sharing, in making and creating"* **(Pinkola, 1992).**

THROUGH ALL OF THE HEALING WORK YOU DO, YOU WILL DO the most important thing for yourself to nurture your inner child. Cultivating a healthy relationship with your inner child will lead to compassion for them and your adult self. It will also teach you how to love every part of yourself and appreciate who you are. Your inner child holds the key to living in the present moment. Children don't worry about the past or the future. They are aware that the moment they are experiencing is the only one worth focusing on. As a result, they notice more about the world around them than adults do. When you grow up, you forget to enjoy the smell of freshly cut grass or notice how blue the sky is. The little moments in life that can bring us so much joy are forgotten about and replaced by worry, stress, and self-doubt. Reconnect with your inner child so that you can help them to heal the neglected inner child. Offer them love and support as you guide them out of the darkness and into the light. Allow your inner child to resurface and guide you to do things you haven't done in years. You may find yourself becoming more playful. It's healthy to allow your inner child to come out to play and show you the joy for life that you have been missing. This will make any healing that you're going through easier. If you can find joy in little moments, the tough moments don't seem so heavy. You will be able to carry the weight of your problems with ease, knowing that you're capable of solving them and returning to your natural state of joy. Living in the present moment and feeling joy for the wonders of the world was your natural state before limiting beliefs and adult responsibilities got in the way. Let's look at three ways you can reconnect with your inner child and develop a healthy relationship with yourself that is full of compassion and love.

Hypnotherapy

A fantastic way to connect with your inner child is through hypnotherapy. This can lead to positive changes in the adult as the inner child heals. Hypnotherapy can encourage self-love, compassion, and positive self-talk. Inner child hypnosis uses various tools and techniques to access, communicate with, calm, and support your inner child (Coleman, n.d.). If you're finding it hard to communicate with your inner child using the other methods, perhaps hypnotherapy is for you. You may have gone through a lot in your life, and it can be hard to access these traumatic memories on your own sometimes. With the support of a therapist, you can meet your inner child and form a healthy relationship with them. Your therapist will spend the first couple of sessions building trust with you and speaking about your early life so that by the time they dive into your subconscious, you feel safe and comfortable. Part of the process involves conscious cognitive dialogue, which means that negative self-talk is replaced with positive self-talk. When you're under hypnosis, suggestions will be made by your therapist that can encourage you to let go of the fear and anxiety that your inner child is feeling. They will help you change the limiting beliefs you formed from this fear and replace them with positive thoughts about yourself. You may travel back to the memory that caused trauma for you and caused a limiting belief to form. Still, you will do so knowing that your therapist is there to protect you and help you to face the fear and soothe your inner child.

We know that the shadow self is formed by the neglected inner child and that the shadow self is made up of the subconscious and unconscious minds. It makes sense to use hypnotherapy to heal something unconscious. Getting straight to the core of the issue by entering your subconscious mind may help you heal faster. You may also experience less emotional pain when you need to revisit traumatic memories to heal because you have a therapist to talk to about it afterward. Hypnosis can help you heal emotional pain and overcome self-sabotage that started due to childhood trauma that was never addressed. When you heal your inner child, you will build your confidence and self-esteem. Having a hypnotherapist by your side to help you calm your anxieties and fears as you journey into self-love can only be helpful. Part of your journey may be learning to accept help from others. This may be something you need to do to cultivate self-love and compassion. In this case, the best thing you could do for yourself would be hypnotherapy. Be kind to yourself, my friend. Listen to what your inner child needs. You know in your heart what you need best and which healing method will resonate with you. Run towards it with love and optimism, and you won't go wrong.

Self-Compassion

Learning to have compassion for yourself involves having compassion for your inner child and the things they went through. The first step is to acknowledge that you do not need to fix yourself. You're perfect the way you are. We all started as beautiful souls who were free and playful. Still, life throws expectations at us and new responsibilities as we get older, which means we have to leave that fun behind. Now that you can see which experiences have formed your shadow self and led to problems in your life, it's time to have compassion for the fact this happened to you in the first place. You deserve to let go of the burden and feel that spark of joy that you left behind in your childhood. Your inner child may have let that spark go out at the exact moment that they felt neglected and formed the shadow self. Travel back to that moment with them through visualization or meditation. Have compassion because you had to deal with such a heavy emotion at such a young age, and realize that you did the best that you could. Understand the situation from your inner child's perspective. Whatever you experienced must have been much more terrifying for a child than an adult. Give yourself a break. You are so much stronger than you give yourself credit for. It's time to offer yourself the compassion that you provide to others. Here are some ways you can practice compassion for yourself in your daily life.

1. Practice forgiveness. Stop blaming yourself for past mistakes to break the pattern and stop blaming yourself for future ones. Mistakes are part of being human. It's how you learn and grow.
2. Adopt a growth mindset whereby challenges are an opportunity to grow rather than something to be feared.
3. Express gratitude for how far you have gotten already in your healing journey and all you have overcome in your life.

4. Be mindful of your thoughts. Ban self-judgment. Silence your inner critic and allow yourself to feel appreciation for the fact that you're a unique human being.

Self-Love

Self-love can be achieved by parenting your inner child. Love for our inner child will lead to self-love in this present moment. Offer your inner child the love that you would offer to any child. Support their dreams and praise their talents. What did you like to do as a child? Rather than criticize yourself for still having a desire to paint a wall with your hands or run barefoot through the grass, just allow it. Permit yourself to do the things that will bring your joy without any judgment. Don't worry about others judging you either. If they knew the secret to feeling immense joy was to let their inner child out to play and run wild, they would do it too. Laughter can be very healing for your mind, body, and soul. Allow your inner child to guide you in whichever direction they want to go, and just follow the joy. Give yourself some relief from all of your hard work because you deserve it. Whenever something from the past does come up to be healed, you need to love that part of yourself too. Self-love is more than appreciating what you like about yourself. It involves looking at the personality traits you don't like and the mistakes you wish you didn't make and accepting that they are part of who you are. We all have flaws, and this is what makes us unique. The very trait that you do not like about yourself could be something that somebody else admires in you. Acceptance of all that you are will open your heart to self-love purely and honestly. Rejecting parts of you that you do not like will not allow you to hold on to a healthy love for yourself. You will find that you can use the mirror exercise mentioned in chapter 11 to cultivate self-love too. Switch the exercise around. The next time you admire something about somebody, see if you can notice how the very thing you admire is also within you. You will start to notice that the universe is mirroring you. You cannot see something positive in somebody else that you don't possess yourself. The more self-love that you cultivate, the more your relationships will change for the better too. When you learn to love yourself for everything you are, including your flaws, you will love other people in this same way. This will bring you closer to them and improve both of your lives. Here are some ways that you can practice self-love in your daily life:

1. Stop comparing yourself to others. You're different for a reason. Embrace the fact that there is nobody else like you on the planet.
2. Allow yourself to make mistakes. Don't criticize yourself every time you make a mistake. You're allowed to mess up sometimes.
3. Walk away from toxic people and situations. If you notice that a person or situation is encouraging self-doubt instead of self-love, it's ok to walk away.
4. Put yourself first. Make sure that you're content and cared for before you care for others.
5. Be kind to yourself. Buy yourself that new book you wanted. Have a bubble bath. Eat the chocolate cake. You deserve to feel good.
6. Allow yourself to feel your entire range of emotions without judgment. Your emotions will help you to understand yourself.

Conclusion

Now that we have completed the journey to healing your shadow self, you're ready to become your best self. Well done for seeing this through and making it out the other side. By integrating your shadow self into your light, you're giving yourself the gift of becoming whole. The only way to truly step into your power is to understand what it is that you're hiding from yourself in your shadow and then heal it. Exploring your repressed emotions to resolve them is not an easy thing to do. It involves reaching into the darkest parts of your psyche — the parts you wanted to forget about — and dragging them into the light to be seen and heard. Hopefully, you have unveiled positive aspects of your shadow self along the way and discovered gifts and talents long forgotten about. Use these gifts and talents to reconnect with your inner child often and continue to heal any shadow aspects that may arise from this point forward. It's important to note that while you will have already done a lot of healing if you followed the exercises in this book, you still have a long way to go. Healing is never finished. Once we understand and accept this, we understand what it is to be human. You will start to notice what your emotional triggers are presented more frequently,

Conclusion

and it will be easy to tell when you're projecting. Although your healing is never done and never should be done, it will get easier if you're living life to the fullest with all of its joy and all of its lessons.

The exercises in this book were designed to come back to them any time you need to. The meditations, journaling, mirroring, and inner dialogue exercises will help you to process any new parts of your shadow that rise up as you go deeper into yourself and become more self-aware. Remember that the key to all inner work is self-love. Working with your inner child will help you cultivate self-love for yourself and hold compassion for yourself throughout your life. You deserve to feel free and joyful. Use everything that you now know, and always trust your intuition. You're a brave and soulful warrior who can get through any storm. As always, be kind to yourself. Remember, you're a beautiful, unique soul on a lifelong journey of healing and discovery. May your light shine brighter as you proceed on your journey a little wiser and a little more conscious than before.

References

Anderson, O. (2016). Personal revolutions: A short course in realness. CreateSpace Independent Publishing Platform, 2016.

Attard, A. (2020, November 4). Repressing emotions: 10 ways to reduce emotional avoidance. PositivePsychology.com. https://positivepsychology.com/repress-emotions/

Bachelard, G. (1971). The poetics of reverie: childhood, language, and the cosmos. Beacon Press.

Blogger, G. (2019, September 16). What is shadow work? Centre of excellence. https://www.centreofexcellence.com/what-is-shadow-work/

Bowe, S. (2019, April 25). Shadow mirror work: Growing from difficult people. Wildfire wisdom | Sue Bowe. https://suebowe.com/shadow-mirror-work/

Brian Tracy. (2018, December 12). The power of your subconscious mind | Brian Tracy. Brian Tracy's self improvement & professional development blog. https://www.briantracy.com/blog/personal-success/understanding-your-subconscious-mind/

Carl Jung and the shadow: Profound quotes and passages.

References

(2017, October). Academy of ideas. https://academyofideas.com/2017/10/carl-jung-shadow-profound-quotes/

Coleman, E. R. (2018). Healing your inner child. Mindworks hypnotherapy. https://mindworkshypnotherapy.com/index.php/resources/applications/inner-child-hypnosis/

Cousins, L. E. (2017). Why "bottling it up" can be harmful to your health | HCF. Hcf.com.au. https://www.hcf.com.au/health-agenda/body-mind/mental-health/downsides-to-always-being-positive

Fletcher, J. (2019, February 12). 4-7-8 breathing: How it works, benefits, and uses. Www.medicalnewstoday.com. https://www.medicalnewstoday.com/articles/324417

Hammond, C. (2018). Shadow work: How to confront your hidden dark side (2020 Guide). Www.world-of-Lucid-Dreaming.com. https://www.world-of-lucid-dreaming.com/shadow-work.html

Holistic Psychologist, T. (2019, May 20). What is the inner child? Www.youtube.com. https://www.youtube.com/watch?v=8ZlDE_ediK0

https://www.briantracy.com/blog/author/brian-tracy. (2017, August 18). The role your subconscious mind plays in your everyday life. Brian Tracy's self improvement & professional development blog. https://www.briantracy.com/blog/personal-success/subconscious-mind-everyday-life/

Idowu Koyenikan. (2016). Wealth for all: living a life of success at the edge of your ability. Grandeur Touch, Llc.

Jacobson, S. (2015, October 22). Everyone else's fault? How to stop projecting feelings onto others. Harley TherapyTM blog. https://www.harleytherapy.co.uk/counselling/how-to-stop-projecting-feelings.htm

Jacobson, S. (2017, March 23). What is the inner child? Harley TherapyTM blog. https://www.harleytherapy.co.uk/counselling/what-is-the-inner-child.htm

Jeffrey, S. (2019, April 15). Shadow work: A complete

guide to getting to know your darker half. Scott Jeffrey. https://scottjeffrey.com/shadow-work/

Jung, C. G. (2018). Quotable Jung. Princeton University Pres.

Kendra Cherry. (2019). How meditation impacts your mind and body. Verywell mind. https://www.verywellmind.com/what-is-meditation-2795927

King, S. (2017, April 25). Are you emotionally repressed? How to tell. Harley TherapyTM blog. https://www.harleytherapy.co.uk/counselling/emotionally-repressed-signs.htm

Lindberg, S. (2018, September 14). It's not me, it's you: Projection explained in human terms. Healthline; Healthline media. https://www.healthline.com/health/projection-psychology

Lopes, C. (2020, June 9). What is shadow work? [5 effective ways to do it!]. Www.youtube.com. https://www.youtube.com/watch?v=5kDN7g9kBAs

Maltz, M., & Powers, M. (2010). Psycho-cybernetics : a new way to get more living out of life. Wilshire Book Co.

Mcgahan, K. (2015). Jack McAfghan : Reflections on life with my master. Kate Mcgahan.

Murphy, J. (2019). The power of your subconscious mind: the complete original edition, plus bonus material. St. Martin's Essentials.

Nordby, J. (2016). Blessed are the weird : a manifesto for creatives. Manifesto Publishing House.

Othon, J. E. (2017, October 20). Carl Jung and the shadow: The ultimate guide to the human dark side. HighExistence. https://highexistence.com/carl-jung-shadow-guide-unconscious/

Peer, M. (2021, January 1). What is RTT? | About rapid transformational therapy and hypnotherapy. Rapid Transformational Therapy: RTT®. https://rtt.com/whatisrtt/

Pinkola, C. (1992). Women who run with the wolves:

References

Myths and stories of the wild woman archetype. Ballantine Books.

Plata, M. (2018, October 31). How to spot your emotional triggers | Psychology today Ireland. Www.psychologytoday.com. https://www.psychologytoday.com/ie/blog/the-gen-y-psy/201810/how-spot-your-emotional-triggers

Raypole, C. (2020, March 31). Repressed emotions: Finding and releasing them. Healthline. https://www.healthline.com/health/repressed-emotions#releasing-them

Richo, D. (2014). How to be an adult in relationships: The five keys to mindful loving. Shambhala.

S Kelley Harrell, & Pratt, C. (2004). Gift of the dreamtime: awakening to the divinity of trauma. Soul Intent Arts.

Shakespeare, W., & Kermode, F. (1998). The tempest. T. Nelson & Sons.chapter

Sue. (2021). Reiki | Holistic heaven - Reiki waves. ReikiWaves.com. http://reiki-waves.com/treatments/reiki/

Tony, T. (2017, February 9). 6 strategic tips to reprogram your mind | Tony Robbins. Tonyrobbins.com. https://www.tonyrobbins.com/mind-meaning/how-to-reprogram-your-mind/

Young, G. (2020, January 3). The relationship between our shadow self & our inner child | Gigi Young. Www.youtube.com. https://www.youtube.com/watch?v=vMrFj9mofrQ&t=14s

Z, M. (2017, September 22). How to know when you're projecting. Happinessclinic. https://www.thehappinessclinic.org/single-post/how-to-know-when-youre-projecting

About the Author

Monique Joiner Siedlak is a writer, witch, and warrior on a mission to awaken people to their greatest potential through the power of storytelling infused with mysticism, modern paganism, and new age spirituality. At the young age of 12, she began rigorously studying the fascinating philosophy of Wicca. By the time she was 20, she was self-initiated into the craft, and hasn't looked back ever since. To this day, she has authored over 50 books pertaining to the magick and mysteries of life.

To find out more about Monique Joiner Siedlak artistically, spiritually, and personally, feel free to visit her **official website**.

www.mojosiedlak.com

facebook.com/mojosiedlak
twitter.com/mojosiedlak
instagram.com/mojosiedlak
pinterest.com/mojosiedlak
bookbub.com/authors/monique-joiner-siedlak

More Books by Monique

African Spirituality Beliefs and Practices
Hoodoo
Seven African Powers: The Orishas
Cooking for the Orishas
Lucumi: The Ways of Santeria
Voodoo of Louisiana
Haitian Vodou
Orishas of Trinidad
Connecting With Your Ancestors
Blood Magic
The Orishas

Practical Magick
Wiccan Basics
Candle Magick
Wiccan Spells
Love Spells
Abundance Spells
Herb Magick
Moon Magick
Creating Your Own Spells

Gypsy Magic
Protection Magick
Celtic Magick

Get a Handle on Life
Stress Management
Get a Handle on Anxiety
Get a Handle on Depression
Get a Handle on Procrastination

Divination Magic for Beginners
Divination with Runes: A Beginner's Guide to Rune Casting

The Yoga Collective
Yoga for Beginners
Yoga for Stress
Yoga for Back Pain
Yoga for Weight Loss
Yoga for Flexibility
Yoga for Advanced Beginners
Yoga for Fitness
Yoga for Runners
Yoga for Energy
Yoga for Your Sex Life
Yoga to Beat Depression and Anxiety
Yoga for Menstruation
Yoga to Detox Your Body
Yoga to Tone Your Body

A Natural Beautiful You
Creating Your Own Body Butter
Creating Your Own Body Scrub
Creating Your Own Body Spray

Last Chance
Join My Newsletter!

If you missed it, I have a free gift available for you and wanted to remind you it's still available.

mojosiedlak.com/self-help-and-yoga-newsletter

Thank you for reading my book.
I really appreciate all your feedback and would love to hear what you have to say! Please leave your review at your favorite retailer!

Made in the USA
Coppell, TX
07 January 2022

71163113R00066